Whispers in the Wind

Jay Rose Ana

Mini Poetry Press

Whispers in the Wind
Jay Rose Ana

Copyright © 2022 Jay Rose Ana

The author asserts the moral right under the Copyright, Designs and Patents Act 1988 to be identified as the author of this work.

All rights reserved. No part of this publication may be reproduced, stored in a retrieval system, or transmitted, in any form or by any means without the prior written consent of the author, nor be otherwise circulated in any form of binding or cover other than that in which it is published and without a similar condition being imposed on the subsequent purchaser.

ISBN 978-1-915787-06-4

Cover Design by Martin Driscoll

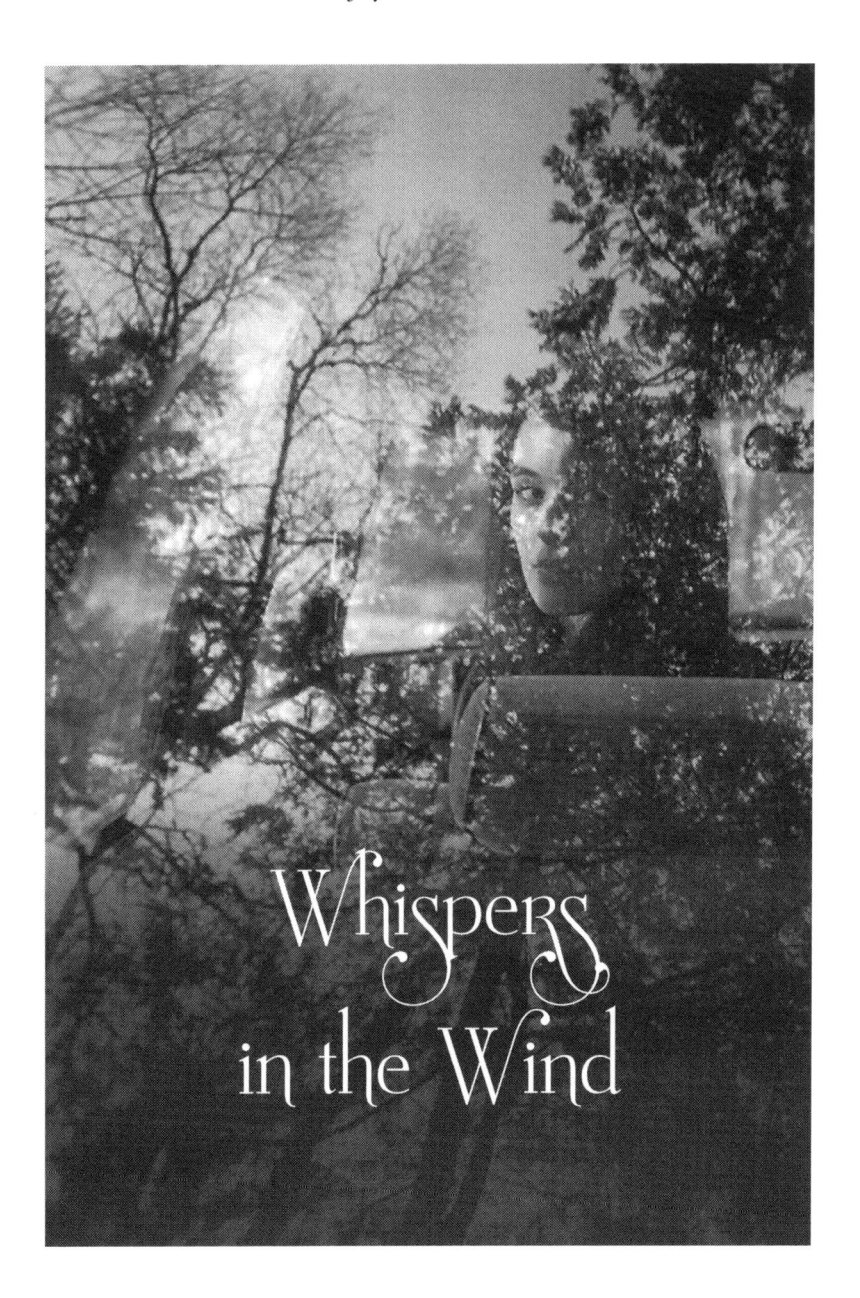

Whispers in the Wind
Jay Rose Ana

Whispers in the Wind

Whispers in the Wind
Jay Rose Ana

Whispers in the Wind
Jay Rose Ana

DEDICATION

This autobiographical poetry collection was hard to write, hard to live, and culminated during a worldwide pandemic. Whispers in the Wind would never have been written if it were not for the love and support of my beautiful family in helping me face demons that once were buried too deeply.

I dedicate this first collection to my children Jessica, Daniel, budding young poet Jacob, and my grandson Joseph. All of whom shared every step of this journey and put up with me whilst I found the words and courage to write of things I never dared speak of before.

And, to Sharon, who keeps the warmth and togetherness in our family during the most challenging of times.

Whispers in the Wind
Jay Rose Ana

Whispers in the Wind
Jay Rose Ana

CONTENTS

PRELUDE "IT BEGINS WITH A WHISPER"	9
ACT ONE "RED FLAGS AND BAYONETS"	15
ACT TWO "PURPLE HEARTS AND CORONETS"	55
ACT THREE "FIRE AMBER AND LIFE CHANGES"	87
ACT FOUR "YELLOW SAPPHIRES OF HOPE"	121
ACT FIVE "GREEN LIGHTS THE WAY FORWARD"	155
EPILOGUE "YOU ARE ENOUGH"	205

Whispers in the Wind
Jay Rose Ana

Whispers in the Wind

PRELUDE

"it begins with a whisper"

Whispers in the Wind
Jay Rose Ana

My best poker face.
Hiding signs of emotion.
Bring me back to life.

Whispers in the Wind
Jay Rose Ana

Whispers in the Wind

She finds comfort deep in wooded forests
Where modernity has yet to infest
Peace embraces amongst splendid crowds
In quietness, amidst perfect creatures loud

She finds respite beneath life's weary tree
Strong branches cradle purposefully
Whispers on breeze, nature converses free
No longer subjects of urban hyperbole

She rests a while beneath shades canopy
Sweetly enveloped by Earths leafy tree
Dreaming as nature washes over her
She connects again, nature's whisperer

Connected with Earth she feels once again
Releasing, at last, her life-long pain
Hopeful skies feel grandly once more
She rises, renewed, ready to explore

Whispers in the Wind
Jay Rose Ana

Are You Okay?

One of life's simplest
questions to ask, yet
one of life's hardest
questions to reply:

Are you okay?

At no other time
do few words, reveal
so much of us and
how we truly feel:

Me? I am fine.

Whispers in the Wind
Jay Rose Ana

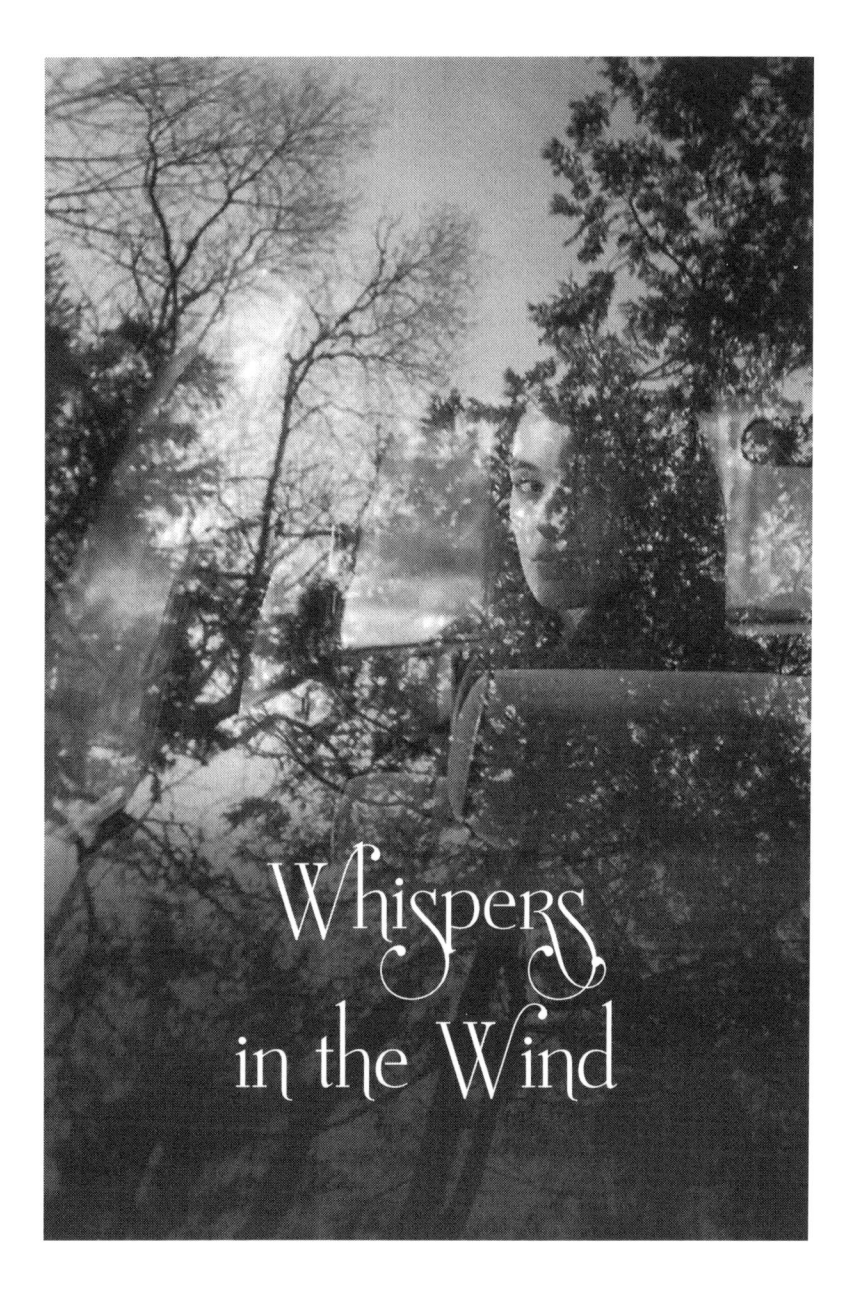

Whispers in the Wind

Whispers in the Wind
Jay Rose Ana

Whispers in the Wind

ACT ONE

"red flags and bayonets"

Whispers in the Wind
Jay Rose Ana

Dear heart and brain, I
admit I have a problem.
Please be one, again.

Whispers in the Wind
Jay Rose Ana

ACT ONE

BOTTLETOP RUNWAY	21
SMILING DEPRESSION	22
HOPELESS HOURS	23
INSTEAD, SHE WEEPS	25
CRADLE OF SHAME	29
HOT AIR BALLOON	30
A DARK THOUGHT	32
HIDDEN TREASURE	33
POOL OF TEARS	35
DO THE SCARS SHOW?	38
EVERYTHING HAS ITS PLACE	40
TIME IS A HEALER	41
EVERYONE DIES TWICE	43
THE CANVAS WEEPS	45
A GOOD PLACE	51
A GUIDING HAND	52

Whispers in the Wind
Jay Rose Ana

Whispers in the Wind
Jay Rose Ana

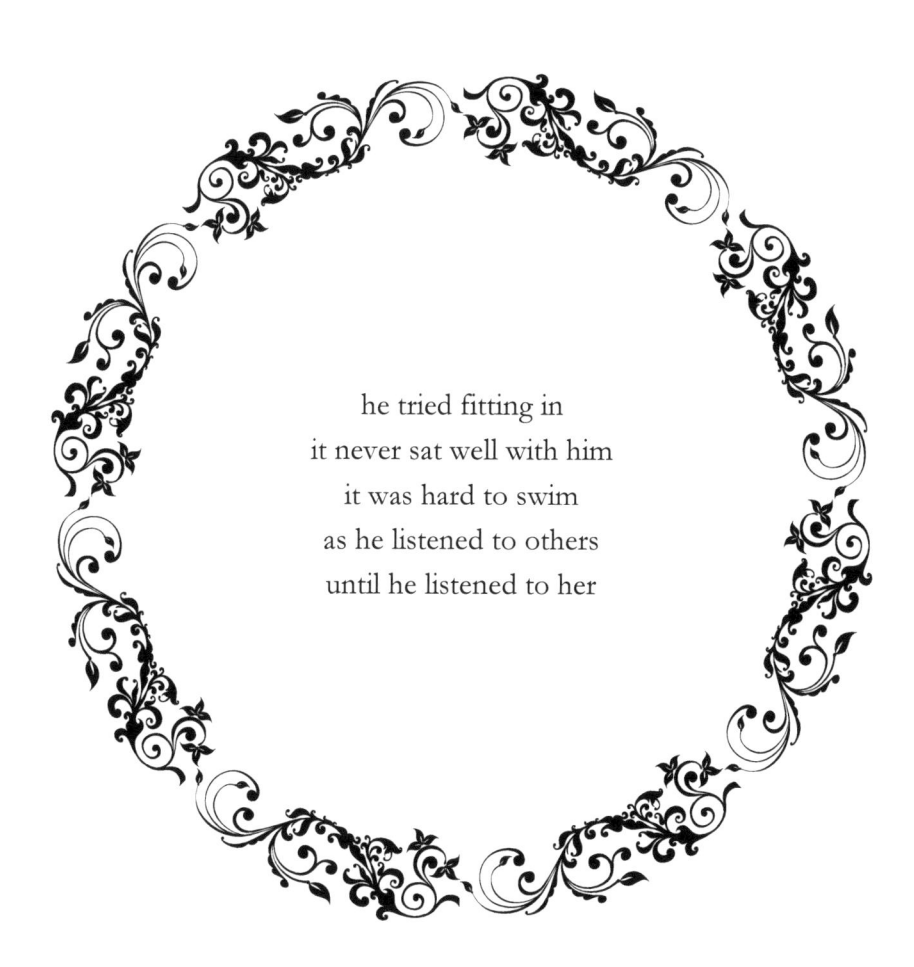

he tried fitting in
it never sat well with him
it was hard to swim
as he listened to others
until he listened to her

Whispers in the Wind
Jay Rose Ana

Whispers in the Wind
Jay Rose Ana

Bottletop Runway

Glass shards piercing skin, bloodletting in, the basement of the club, amidst laughter and a single rubber glove.

Early mornings without care, sorting broken glass bottles, each five pence in return for a dare, they slept there.

Lids discarded but not for them, their bottle-top runway, sunless but not for them, dancing carefree, becoming we.

No window observed days blue sky become grey as their sun shone into dark late nights, and one head still fights.

Echoes of them still resound, without their sound, shards of glass feel sharper now, bottom of barrels never found.

So long ago now, still one heart beating, seeping, thoughts weeping, into the bottom of an empty discarded glass.

Bottle-top runway days would never end. Upon two hearts they depend. So long ago now, wondering why, and how.

One friend, one love, one runways end.

Whispers in the Wind
Jay Rose Ana

Smiling Depression

I am good, fabulous in fact.
Couldn't be better, wholly intact.
Check my social, see how I smile.
Bet you haven't seen anyone,
together like this for a while.

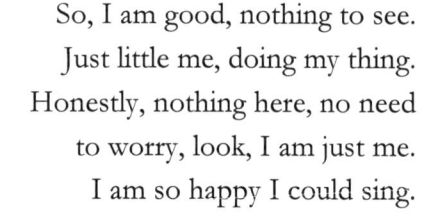

        So, I am good, nothing to see.
        Just little me, doing my thing.
        Honestly, nothing here, no need
        to worry, look, I am just me.
        I am so happy I could sing.

Do I need someone to listen?
To me? Hell no! I am just fine
the way I am. I keep myself
to myself though, don't worry if I
seem a bit dull, my glass is half-full.

        Because nobody gives a damn.
        About me, you see, who *I* am.
        I am sorry, I didn't mean
        to speak that thought out loud.
        Every silver lining has its cloud.

Whispers in the Wind
Jay Rose Ana

Hopeless Hours

when hopeless hours chime there
when despair takes a lonely chair
when darkness blinds brighter light
when day becomes blackest night

she lays awake, silently still,
empty bottles beside her windowsill
each morning sun blacker still
life hanging on its final will

that final moment finds her still,
time to pay life's heavy bill,
she grips tightly on to woven scorn
to cast her hopeless 'til its shorn

Whispers in the Wind
Jay Rose Ana

facing fear with fear itself
as hopeless falls from dusty shelf
reborn, she can longer fall
filling her eyes with rage once more

pushing hopeless through hopeful's door
raging fiercely on for war
she shambles firmly into night
her hopeless heart takes hopeful flight

once more unto the early hour
loving memories overpower
and in that final lasting sight
she casts her hopes unto the night

she casts them wide, she casts them far
drifting on nights breezy star
to beds of waking colourful flowers
to comfort others in hopeless hours

Whispers in the Wind
Jay Rose Ana

Instead, She Weeps

Midnight. She tries to sleep.

She wonders what shape her life will take.
As she lays upon her bed awake.
Dreaming on clouds passing in night.
Wending their way, kissed by moonlight.

She wonders if they look down upon.
And see all things she could become.
As they pass by in starry sky.
Gathering hopes until they cry.

Two AM. There she is again.

Laying in bed for several hours.
Going over again, playing card towers.

Holding her breath so it doesn't topple.
Trying to make sense like she's Aristotle.
As the earth spins away.

Whispers in the Wind
Jay Rose Ana

Its foot stuck on its throttle.

Chased by thunder. It makes her wonder.
She clenches dreams, catches burning steam.
Drifting far into places she has never been.

🍃

Three AM. She needs an Amen.

Hoping for love and stupid things.
She'll take what you've got, what happiness brings.

Making promises she will never keep.
To close her eyes and fall asleep.
And not wake up, but instead, she weeps.

Tears drown her soul, a river deep.
Feeding clouds there up high.
Wondering if, they wonder why.
Bottle-tops serenade a lullaby.

🍃

Four AM. A strange omen.

Pacing at night along dark halls.

Whispers in the Wind
Jay Rose Ana

Fearing shadows as morning calls.

Creaking under foot she keeps on moving.
Endlessly consuming endless disapproving.
All for naught, sleep not improving.

Reaching dreams edge, feeling cheap.
Deep rivers beckon, she takes a leap.
She prays up high, her soul to keep.

Five AM. Her nightly requiem.

One day, one night, here or there.
Time doesn't matter, place doesn't care.

She promises there, she will prevail.
One way or another, escape her jail.
Clouds keep her tears as she exhales.

Six AM. Wondering when.

She needs to trust herself to sleep.
Until it comes, instead, she weeps.

Whispers in the Wind
Jay Rose Ana

And says tomorrow she will try again.
Face distant drums, come sun or rain.
She is sure this promise, she will keep.
Though yet again, instead, she weeps.

As she lays on her bed wide awake.
Wondering what shape her life will take.

Dreaming on clouds passing in night.
Wending their way, kissed by moonlight.

She wonders if they look down upon.
See all the things she could become.

To close her eyes and fall asleep.
And not wake up, but instead, she weeps.

Whispers in the Wind
Jay Rose Ana

Cradle of Shame

Dreaming under moonlight.
Overthinking under starlight.
One finger to love's Moon.
Too bright amidst her gloom.
As clouds hurry on by.
Cries a slow lullaby.

Hoping for tomorrow.
Winds of change blow sorrow.
Through lost night-time hours.
Misty cold falling rain showers.
Washes away life's pain.
But she'll never be the same.

Painful memories remain.
Facing life once again.
Beneath faded starlight.
Reflecting in moonlight.
The candle burns its flame.
In her cradle of shame.

Whispers in the Wind
Jay Rose Ana

Hot Air Balloon

Some days, she feels like a hot air balloon.
Some days, she is holding life's rope.
Some days, she feels like soaring up high.
Some days, well, she just can't cope.

On days she dreams of floating proud.
She fills her world with hope.
On days when she feels tied to ground.
It is all she can do to cope.

Days afloat are when she is found.
Anxiety and fear elope.
On days when her fears abound.
She clings to slippery slopes.

Some days she looks to clouds in skies.
Some days her head falls and cries.
Some days she wonders if she belongs.
Some days she fears she may not be strong.

Whispers in the Wind
Jay Rose Ana

Some days she feels like yes, yes, yes.
Some days she retreats with no.
Days when fear outweighs hope.
Are days when strong winds blow.

It is in those winds she really knows.
How well she can truly cope.
It is not fear of holding the rope.
Her fear is letting it go.

Whispers in the Wind
Jay Rose Ana

A Dark Thought

It passed momentarily through her mind,
in all but the briefest of time, and yet
she knew, deep in there, dark thoughts she would find.

She knows better, she does, to let thoughts swirl.
So, she thought, of that thought, as a small grape
on strong vine, green fields, of beautiful wine.

She thought a while of little seeds in that
tiny grape, and of new life it would bring.

That thought hit her again, indeed take hold.
In chilly air, hairs of her neck stretched out,
as her warm summer thoughts twist icy cold.

I have power of life in my mind.
And deep dark thoughts I admit I find.

Would anyone know? Would anyone care?
Of that thought swirling black inside of there?

Whispers in the Wind
Jay Rose Ana

Hidden Treasure

Her picture holds a thousand lies.
Lies that bind, binds that are blind.
She digs deeper, deeper, to find,
her truth, her core, the bedrock of her mine.

The breathing red heart, the poisoned chalice.
The sleeping dragon, the shot that killed Alice.

Buried somewhere, in the deep confined,
that treasured thing, peace of mind.
But nothing is free, there will be a cost.
The risk she takes, her sanity lost.

A dying heart, a dragon slayed,
an empty chalice, an eternal maze.

Spiralling down, tumbling through,
no handhold in sight, will she ever breakthrough?
How deep is this cavern? Only time will tell.
The truth she yearns, her personal hell.

Whispers in the Wind
Jay Rose Ana

A stone-cold heart, dragon bones,
a dusty cup, and still she roams.

Broken and shattered, her treasures scattered.
She hits stony ground hard, body marred.
An unusual rock, an archaeological find.
She has been this way before, her path undefined.

What is going on?
Where did she fall?

There, in the ground, she finds a picture, of her.
Deep in her mind, memories stir.
She remembers now, she sees it all.
But can no longer stand, she can barely crawl.

Will anyone hear?
The silence of her call?

The discovery made, the answer she seeks.
From deep within, painful truth shrieks.
Deaths' hand outstretched, demands a soul.
Her journeys end, the price of the toll.

Whispers in the Wind
Jay Rose Ana

Pool of Tears

Sometimes, I wonder,
Where love really is?
Headlong down a rabbit hole.
No wonderland here.

A familiar tune.
The words unclear.
Like a half-remembered song.
Half-joy, half-tears, all-fear.

Drinking the potion.
From a metre to a mile.
Does not really matter.
When an empty vial.

Going through the motions.
Search for it still.
Like the Cheshire Cat, just out of reach.
Always remaining, over the hill.

Whispers in the Wind
Jay Rose Ana

"You must first find yourself", says Hatter.
"Then let time unfold".
"For a story without love".
"Remains a story untold!"

🍃

Laughing in the distance.
The Queen stole a heart.
Toying with persistence.
Keeping hope and love apart.

🍃

Reciting, Mock Turtle.
Withdraws into its shell.
Melancholy poetry.
It bids so long, farewell.

🍃

So, it is back to the surface.
To the dirt and the stone.
And a time-watching rabbit.
Standing astride of a hole.

🍃

Whispers in the Wind
Jay Rose Ana

"It is getting very late", it says.
With a disapproving glare.
But time goes by slowly.
When one cries in despair.

Searching, never ending,
looking under everywhere.
Down every rabbit hole.
Where it leads, who knows where?

So, sometimes, I wonder.
Where does love, really live?
But love is not something to seek.
Love is something to give.

Whispers in the Wind
Jay Rose Ana

Do the Scars Show?

Do the scars show, can you even tell?
No longer always, as I have ever been.
You should, you know, you put me through hell.

Diving deep, holding breath, doing well?
Surviving threats, discovering my own queen.
Do the scars show, can you even tell?

Each spiteful word, a hateful spell.
Your spit, did you know, leaves me stained and unclean.
You should, you know, you put me through hell.

Frozen by time. I no longer feel.
A tragedy played out, badly, scene by scene.
Do the scars show, can you even tell?

Whispers in the Wind
Jay Rose Ana

Do you know? I tried, to rise, but fell.
Nobody can decide, hide, within their gene.
You should, you know, you put me through hell.

But I have found the courage to last the bell.
To navigate torrents of the in-between.

Do the scars show, can you even tell?
You should, you know, you put me through hell.

Whispers in the Wind
Jay Rose Ana

Everything has its Place

She was told everything has its place and
everything has its time.

But she wonders of the overlap, the space
between worlds, beneath dirt and grime.

When is the right time for pain,
and where is the right place for loss?

And what happens when worlds collide,
and she falls to ground with no more tears to cry?

What of time then? And what of place?
What of where? And what of when?

As you rest, she needs to remember,
the smooth of your skin, the curve of your smile.

And each, and every, contour
of your beautiful face.

Whispers in the Wind
Jay Rose Ana

Time is a Healer

Time's a great healer. Really, what a croc!
Time's good for nothing, 'cept in cuckoo clocks.
Reaching deep inside, stirring up deep below.
Demons bubble up, teasing things only they know.

Contaminated, feeling hurts sometimes.
Feeling is healing, digging deep in grime.
Hour by hour, needing a shower.
Minute by minute, reeking deep in it.

Buried in layers, the stench makes her sick.
The secrets so deep, their lies are so thick.
Exhausted, push on. Extorted, put on.
Tick tock, cuckoo clock. Tick tock, tick tock.

Nowhere in the world, would she rather be.
Up to her knees, stained by all she dare see.
Push it back inside, keep it locked away.
Does this help healing? Back away, she says.

Whispers in the Wind
Jay Rose Ana

Back away!

Buried with reason, digging is treason.
What good has it done? Maybe next season.
Flee little birdie, coo your little coo!
Come back this way soon, secrets inside you.

Tick tock.
Time.

Tick tock.
Tick.
Tock.

Whispers in the Wind
Jay Rose Ana

Everyone Dies Twice

Everyone hurts.
Everyone cries.
Everyone loves.
Everyone dies.

Not everyone heals.
Not everyone laughs.
Not everyone lives.
Frozen photographs.

Hearts will always break.
Hope sinks, makes you drown.
Regret keeps nights awake.
Kicks hard when you are down.

Nights will always be dark.
The moon won't always shine.
Life will always feel stark.
When hearts do not align.

Time will always tick.
Candles will always burn.
Pain will always stick.
Love will always yearn.

Friends will come and go.
Memories can be repressed.

Whispers in the Wind
Jay Rose Ana

Lovers may never show.
Faith is all that's left.

The strings will always play.
The bells will always chime.
The piano man will have his day.
The bartender always calls time.

But tomorrow will always come.
Like the beating of a drum.
Hope is there to be found.
And lift you from the ground.

Hope will prop you up.
Hope will hold your hand.
Faith will see you through.
No prayers, no chants, no choral band.

Just belief from a hopeful you.
Believe in you.

Whispers in the Wind
Jay Rose Ana

The Canvas Weeps

Is what I am doing selfish? Is that why I feel alone?
Surrounded by understanding faces.
Making carefully considered spaces.
For them, not me, the different one.

Slowly extracting me from them.
Through the label of assurity.
They whisper inclusion, yet I feel an intrusion.
Into their normality, a juxtaposition of morality.

Some think it a triviality. Some, losing my marbles.
Some call it, tolerance. Some, use transphobic language.
A lexicon, created for people like me by people not like me.
A gift, from the world, thank you so much for describing me.

Another form of labelling.
An abstraction of a human painting.
Framed within an open prison. Solitary. Alone. Disconnected.
Surrounded by human walls of solidarity.

Whispers in the Wind
Jay Rose Ana

I am, for the world to see, a moment in time.
Stillness captured, but I am, and always will be, me.
A dichotomy. So, I smile, and I wonder.
If they will ever see, love between layers of me.

They do look on with appreciation.
For sacrifices they make in the name of we.
But I am no more than a blend of their tones.
Artwork for its colour than meaning.

Sporadically put on show, placed prominently.
Then veiled and left to gather dust.
Just inside glances of passing feet.
Just outside any reach of a heartbeat.

So, dust it is, my only friend.
A unique perspective.
A beautiful never. A lost forever.
A sealed window to a selfish me.

Whispers in the Wind
Jay Rose Ana

There, amongst settled dust.
Life's bright colours fade.
As the hopeful years pass.
It's frame gently splinters.

Over many cold and lonely,
soul dampening winters.
Layers of dust keeps.
As the canvas weeps.

Whispers in the Wind
Jay Rose Ana

'The Canvas Weeps' image by Laura Saul.

Whispers in the Wind

ACT ONE

interlude

Whispers in the Wind
Jay Rose Ana

Whispers in the Wind
Jay Rose Ana

A Good Place

She has no idea what today brings.
No expectations, no control over feelings.
She strives to be her best self today.
No matter what falls into her way.

The world has no idea what today brings.
Forests living in fear, creatures in hiding.
The Earth will turn, living half in dismay.
Doing its best as we cut its resources away.

Humans have no idea what today brings.
Tears, laughter, a single heart that sings.
Her heart is singing, somewhere deep inside.
But today it yearns, for a good place to hide.

A Guiding Hand

when he was young
there was no one
to sit him down
and guide his life

to tell him he could
be anything he wants
to be if he set
his mind to it

He only ever wanted
to be she and for
you to see her so
he set his mind to it

He found her hiding deep in there

And she sat down
and told him
it would be tough
but it will be okay

            one day

Whispers in the Wind
Jay Rose Ana

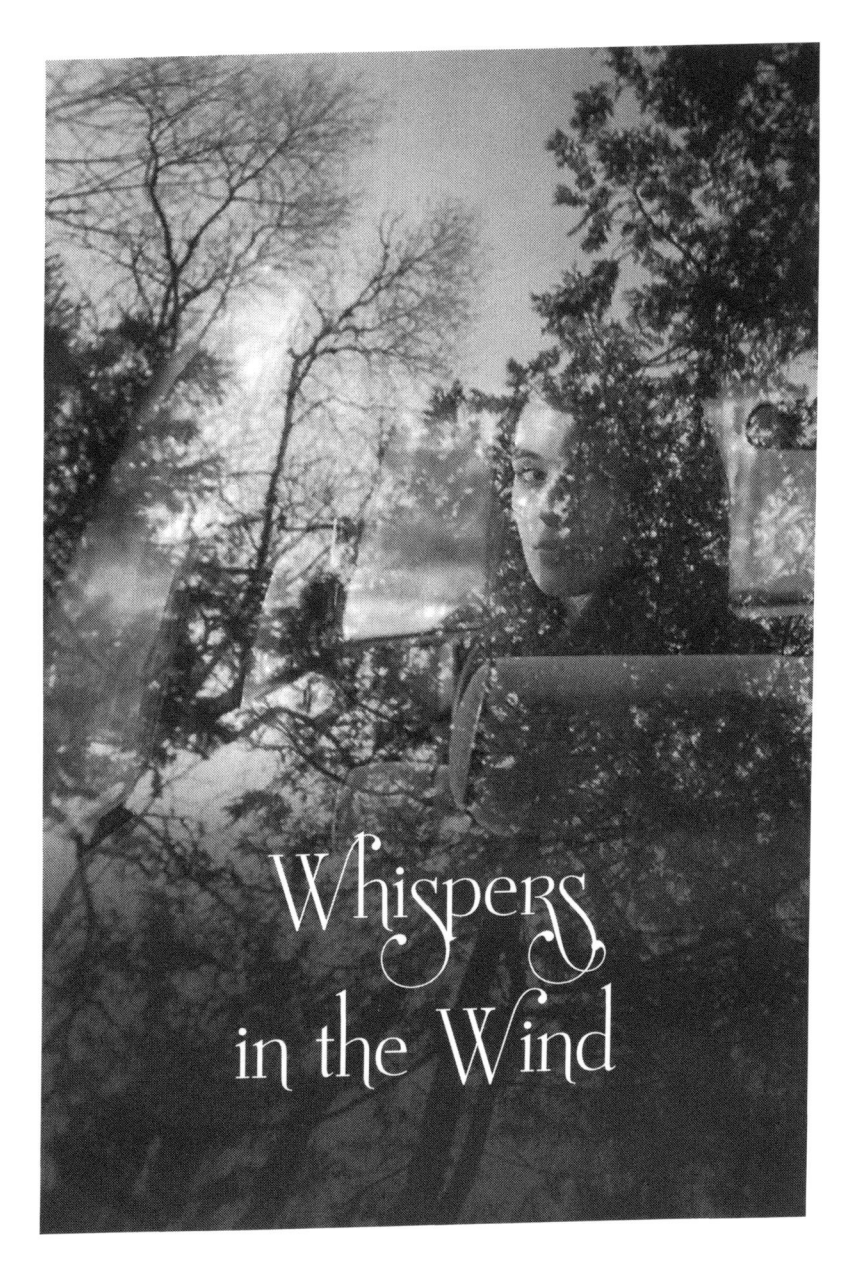

Whispers in the Wind
Jay Rose Ana

Whispers in the Wind

ACT TWO

"purple hearts and coronets"

Whispers in the Wind
Jay Rose Ana

I look inside me.
I do not see what you see.
I do not see me.

Whispers in the Wind
Jay Rose Ana

ACT TWO

LONELY SCREAM	61
DELUGE	62
IMPASTO	63
HER TORTURED SOUL	65
THE DEVIL TO PAY	66
NEW MORNINGS DAWN	69
INVITATION TO HOPE	71
RELIC	72
WHAT IS FAITH?	73
NEVERWHERE	74
ALL SHE FEELS IS WORRY	75
DITTO	76
PORTRAIT OF A BEST FRIEND	77
NATURE'S KINTSUGI	78
BEING DIFFERENT	83
WORDS TO LIVE BY	84

Whispers in the Wind
Jay Rose Ana

Whispers in the Wind
Jay Rose Ana

accepting herself
for whom she is now, always
was so very hard
but she feels so much lighter
like taking off an old coat

Whispers in the Wind
Jay Rose Ana

Whispers in the Wind
Jay Rose Ana

Lonely Scream

There may come a time, she hopes it does.
When our Earth feels a fabulous place.
And those, who made us, there up above.
Can look down again with love and grace.

She hopes freedom will become the way.
Opportunity knocks every hopeful door.
Hate and scorn abandoned, out of place.
Not one person needs to plead for more.

She hopes we become THE human race.
And we learn to live another day.
And that distance brings a happier face.
Equal voice for all, becomes the way.

She lives in hope for all these things.
And we may not achieve everything.
She hopes we try to become this dream.
And put an end to our lonely scream.

Whispers in the Wind
Jay Rose Ana

Deluge

My heart doesn't dance to rain.
Celebrations pop doesn't sweeten champagne.
Shaken bottles don't let their pressure drop.

Through fractured lens of whispering raindrops,
my hearts vessel stops, I know the pop of a bottle top.

Trembling fractals of emotions hurling from heavens commotions,
shattering glass, bottle tops pop, never stop.

Raining, spitting, gushing.
Raging, splatting, flooding.

This sudden cloudburst deluge,
I spill my carbonated heart rouge.

Swamped and smattered, head to toe,
yet the only drop that never stops is

the one that fell,
from me, for you.

Whispers in the Wind
Jay Rose Ana

Impasto

When she is done, and she is gone.
Her portrait will remain.

The craft of your hand.
The focus of your eye.
The steadiness of your breath.
The openness of your mind.

Your expression of her.
Will be an expression of us.

Share in her dreams,
as whispers in air.
Select your canvas,
with extra care.

Whispers in the Wind
Jay Rose Ana

As you paint gently,
let there be no rush.
Layer after layer,
let your colours blend.

A unique palette,
upon your brush.
For the tones you select,
will show the strength of us.

And when you frame this painting,
please take extra care.
For the outside of her, over time,
may require a little repair.

And when you show this painting,
she would like the world to know.
She took a deep breath,
stepped out of the grey.

Into a world of colour.
and lived her life, her way.
Her portrait will remain.

Whispers in the Wind
Jay Rose Ana

Her Tortured Soul

Who is she and where is her heart?
If not at home, then where to start?
Who reaches into her tortured soul?
Who reads the sign she is no longer whole?
Who peeks through her window?
From the world at large.
Revealing unfinished limbo.
Beneath her bright visage.
Who is captivated by her smoky presence?
What bravery seeks her buried essence?
Who believes when doubters cry?
And who remains when others fly?
Who crosses worlds to be the one to get her?
To forge a bond, a world together.
Who builds their home, who lays their path?
Who brings her peace, who calms her wrath?
Who will accept her as she is found?
Who will be her solid ground?
Who will invest in her future past?
Who will be the one?

Built to last.

The Devil to Pay

For God sake someone tell me,
how I spirit away.
These thoughts always haunting me,
tomorrow is another today.

In the street, you probably would not give me,
any particular time of day.
So, time passes slowly,
these thoughts pushed out the way.

But, if you were to tell me,
perhaps, sometime today.
The only day I could have,
would indeed, be yesterday.

Then, to be honest.
I may be inclined to say,
A fond farewell, adieu my friend.
As I gladly slip away.

But I have learned to live life for today,
face every challenge, come what may.

Whispers in the Wind
Jay Rose Ana

And the demons, that come,
I will try to keep them at bay.
Through the passing of time,
Hour by hour, day by challenging day.

I took a deep breath,
blew the cobwebs away.
Through deep falling dust,
I glimpsed new light of day.

Feeling stronger now,
I save nothing for a rainy day.
And I give you my love,
or at least meet you, halfway.

So many years,
time just frittered away.
Time after time,
each an empty bottle day.

Whilst the cat was away,
the mouse didn't play.
The chips simply fell,
wherever they lay.

Whispers in the Wind
Jay Rose Ana

It can take a whole lifetime,
to find out the hard way.
Life is for living,
so, get yours underway!

Forge day after day,
Rome was not built in a day.
But lay a stone, right here, right now.
That is how you pave the way.

The only thing standing,
in one's own way.
Is one's own shadow,
shackled in feet of clay.

In the cold light of day,
do not fritter life away.

Do not wait until tomorrow,
or you will have…

the Devil to pay.

Whispers in the Wind
Jay Rose Ana

New Mornings Dawn

Somewhere in between.
The night and the day.
Is a moment where I am me.
The best me, I would say.

Half-dream, half-awake.
Full of hope, make no mistake.
This sombre dawn pause.
Reveals me, my truth, awake.

The cool of the air.
Through the windows breeze.
The warmth of my bed.
A few more minutes tease.

The tick of my clock.
Marks each passing of time.
I would say in that moment.
I feel just fine.

Whispers in the Wind
Jay Rose Ana

And then in a beat.
It is the start of the day.
Up and away.
To live my life my way.

I take solace in the fact.
If growth turns decay.
A new morning's dawn.
Is but a few hours away.

So, the best place I can think of.
Is the safety of my bed.
Only fools rush in.
Where angels fear to tread.

My safe space, my respite.
The bank of my tears.
I have invested very heavily.
Over my surviving years.

Whispers in the Wind
Jay Rose Ana

Invitation to Hope

Drifting on a breeze, no longer moving with purpose.
A tall empty cup, once full, now still and nervous.
A blank new page, staring up with trepidation.
A still blue sea, making waves of frustration.

Sand under foot, makes way for tired feet.
Warmth of the sun, melts ice, with hope's heat.
A vacuum in space, holds a big empty nothing.
An expressionless face, no need for bluffing.

And yet, I feel, the morning breeze upon my face.
A cup of warm tea soothes the pain and the aches.
Yes, my page is empty, but my pen holds hope.
The sea is abundant and helps me stay afloat.

The sand, a million lifetimes, cradles my feet.
The sun gives me strength, my solar heartbeat.
An empty nothing is an invitation to dream.
There, I am found, wondering where have I been?

Whispers in the Wind
Jay Rose Ana

Relic

Something inside me survived from the past.
Not a valuable keepsake,
   just a fragment for God's sake.

Historically significant in no particular way.
But surface it did, I remember that day.

Looking forward, feeling bright, heading straight,
   but… like a fool…stupidly turning right.

At the corner, by the shop,
   it slapped so hard I had to stop.

I pondered on it as I roamed,
   before anxiously heading home.

Seeping from my head, I had to quickly act,
   filing it away in these poems labelled 'relic',

but the seal…

                                       …has cracked.

Whispers in the Wind
Jay Rose Ana

What is Faith?

To have faith, looks to better tomorrows.
New sunrises promise hopeful new morns.
Not of hopes and dreams that she might borrow.
But of steps she treads on a road well worn.

Having faith is hopeful in heavy rain.
To marvel at rainbows in mornings light.
Finding her strength to rise through pain.
Knowing she can endure, trusting her light.

To have faith, is to see value of heart.
Wisdom, to listen to ageless souls.
And courage, to rise to a world apart.
And forgive, those who made her less than whole.

Whispers in the Wind
Jay Rose Ana

Neverwhere

She likes hushed peace and quiet calm

She finds safety in darkened rooms

Tranquil silences gently sing

Inner peace promotes headroom

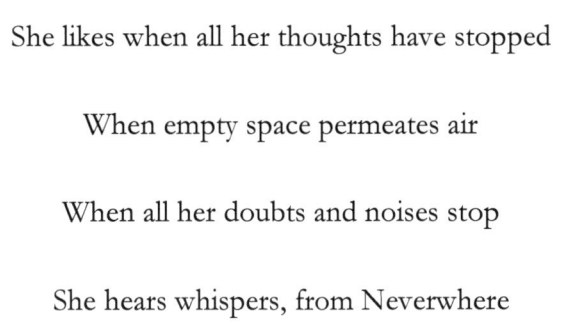

She likes when all her thoughts have stopped

When empty space permeates air

When all her doubts and noises stop

She hears whispers, from Neverwhere

Whispers in the Wind
Jay Rose Ana

All She Feels is Worry

She finds herself in states of anxiousness,
feeling troubled over problems.
There are times to tend to the quality of her inner sense of being.
Worry, and anxiety about worry, exist in pursuit of themselves.

Perpetuating their own existence through memories.
Multiplying in dark places of despair and loneliness.
At these times, she seeks out to comfort another,
and her worry for self, lessens.

When worry strikes, she writes it down, ensures to look
at it tomorrow and asks if it is the real cause of her sorrow.
She could waste her precious life worrying what others may
or may not make of her, but the matter most important of all…

…is what she makes of herself.

Whispers in the Wind
Jay Rose Ana

Ditto

I heard you and I wish I'd said ditto.
So often, hopeless leaves fell from your tree.
Your rustling heart paved Autumn, ditto.
I held your outstretched branches far from me.

To the night sky, to the starlight, ditto.
And to the breeze, to the wind, and the rain.
Whispers in silence cry loudest, ditto.
Longing to hear your sweet voice once again.

I root myself, right here, for you, ditto.
I will be here as you waited for me.
Intertwined branches await your ditto.
Let the moonlight never wane from your tree.

Whispers in the Wind
Jay Rose Ana

Portrait of a Best Friend

…Is an empty box in an art supplies shop.

…A blank canvas where the frame really pops.

…Oil and watercolours aligned neatly unused.

…Not even a brush can stand up accused.

…My best friend died.

…I can't sleep until I've cried.

…The portrait of my best friend will never be said.

…My soul mate will always be dead.

…But their colour will never fade in my head.

…
Whispers in the Wind
Jay Rose Ana

Nature's Kintsugi

She ambles nervously,

through dense woodland.

Lost in the wilderness

of cast-off tenderness.

Lions and jackals ride high,

upon butterflies' wings.

Howling like dark stormy

winds of turbulent days.

Hunting dragonflies,

lancing fireflies, for

nectar concealed deep

within hidden truths.

Whispers in the Wind
Jay Rose Ana

Tender caterpillars
lies stolen enviously
by the too short lives of
unbalanced Mayflies cries.

From a distant viewpoint,
this epic battle for
time and space itself is
fought in a microcosm.

A quiet hum chorus,
cries of pain and need,
lay in desperate need.
Unseen by wider eyes
of hells dark macrocosm.

And yet, the outcome of
this escape from the woods
determines the fate
of the shoulds and the coulds.

Whispers in the Wind
Jay Rose Ana

Bloodlust Jackals howl to

night as sly silent

night-crawlers take up arms

readying black ground tonight.

A full-on ground assault.

Deep in the starry copse,

beside the stagnant pool,

weary travellers fool.

No signpost, no warning,

the lost were never lost

nor were they ever found.

Buried there forever,

below memories ground.

Windows of time blow,

As nature makes it

beautiful once more,

'There you are', words she could only dream of.

Whispers in the Wind

ACT TWO

interlude

Whispers in the Wind
Jay Rose Ana

Whispers in the Wind
Jay Rose Ana

Being Different

Can you see her?
Standing in the crowd.

Can you hear her?
Quietly shouting loud.

Can you spot her?
Standing, proud, and tall.

Can you help her?
If she should fall.

Can you hold her?
When she is sand.

Will you remember her?
Did she help you understand?

Whispers in the Wind
Jay Rose Ana

Words to Live By

Her youngest son.
At the age of nine.
Uttered these words.
She listened to him.

Words to live by.
Words she holds dear.
Childishly simple.
Perfectly clear.

He said…

Be your best you.
Whilst you are alive.

And that was it.

No adult could put it better.
So, she strives to live.
Those words, every day,
to every letter.

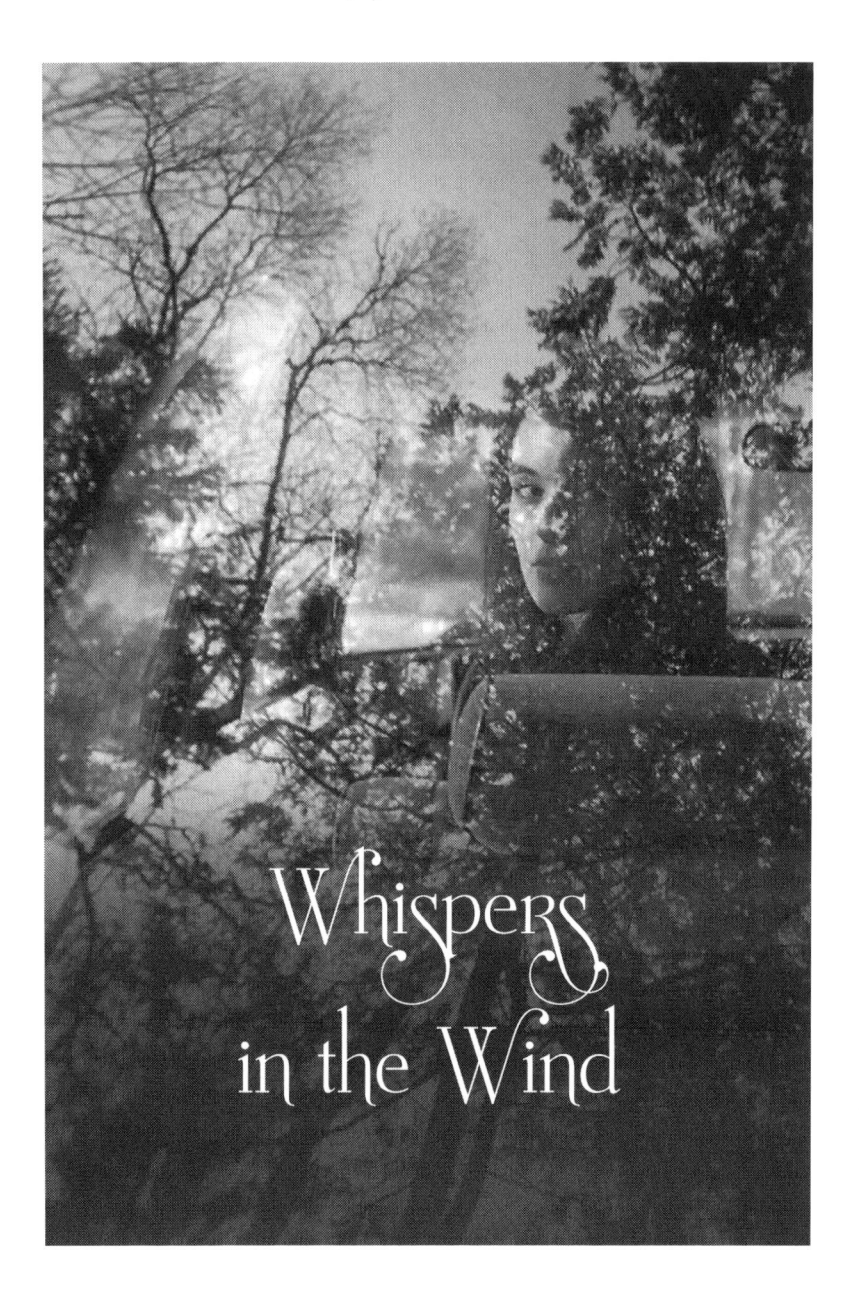

Whispers in the Wind
Jay Rose Ana

Whispers in the Wind
Jay Rose Ana

Whispers in the Wind

ACT THREE

"fire amber and life changes"

Whispers in the Wind
Jay Rose Ana

Grief, battered and bruised.
The one's on the outside healed.
Inside, a mine field.

Whispers in the Wind
Jay Rose Ana

ACT THREE

AMBER FIRES OF HEAVEN	93
CHROMATIC COUNTENANCE	95
HEAVENS PURSE	97
LABYRINTH	98
ANONYMITY	100
TURNING POINT	101
A QUIET PLACE	103
HELL BE WARNED	104
NEVER FITTING IN	106
LIVE, LOVE	107
SOMETIMES	108
BOOK OF LIFE	109
SILENT VOICES	110
YOUR VESUVIUS	111
SAY NO	115
MEMORIES	117

Whispers in the Wind
Jay Rose Ana

Whispers in the Wind
Jay Rose Ana

she finds her own voice
and the strength to just be her
she feels awakened
An open mind to all life
And it feels quite wonderful

Whispers in the Wind
Jay Rose Ana

Whispers in the Wind
Jay Rose Ana

Amber Fires of Heaven

Fire burns in Heaven like it rages through her heart, casting judgement, blazing her hopeful thoughts apart.

Burning sulfur raining from above, like tears only a lonely soul can know. The silent tear, caught, before it wends its way down her face.

Her soul is cast in amber, preserved in state for all time, a time traveller frozen in space, matched with an expressionless face.

Do you judge me, she asked, of the butterfly, rainbow winged as it flew by to meet the sandman in a half-sleepy lullaby.

The whispered return was no, as she fell to her knees, pushed her hands into earth, as the butterfly rested, upturned, beneath the leaf emerging from a small twig of the tree.

Are you a caterpillar, the butterfly enquired in a sleepy whisper, are you preparing to cocoon, if so, you can rest by me.

Whispers in the Wind
Jay Rose Ana

We just met, she replied, and you already know me more than anyone I ever knew. I wish I could cocoon, to become a butterfly like you, I would love to rest a short while here with you.

Two souls rested, she closed her eyes, and fell to sleep, dreaming vivid dreams of nectar and fluttering between slipstreams.

Her companion always just a wing tip away, as they spiralled along the breeze, sometimes slamming upwards, other times drifting down.

We have been together for just a moment, she whispered dreamily, and yet, I feel I know you, like I feel you really know me.

I live, in your world, replied the butterfly, for just a handful of days, but in my world, you are my friend. I have known you for decades.

I was feeling low, said the butterfly, and your dreams lifted me up high, to places I could only imagine travelling with a friend, no longer solo.

The butterfly whispered its last goodbye as she opened her eyes, from the best sleep she ever knew, to find the butterfly cast in amber, a moment, a memory, frozen in space, preserved for all time with a gentle smile upon its face.

Whispers in the Wind
Jay Rose Ana

Chromatic Countenance

I plunge headfirst into new journeys of discovery.
Falling through iridescent hues, energy of starlight, confused.

The gravity of matter in this awkward shape of me.
Blinding ultraviolet rays burning shadows I refuse to face.

Erasing saturation, rising luminescence, a cacophony of hues.
Deafening tones from the raging bull to the silent blues.

Further, I free-fall into spectrums infrared.
Plucking thoughts like guineafowl to sacrificial altars.

Feather by feather ripped from a carcass of a soul never free.
Cherry-popping bursts of fear and doubt consigned to rejection.

Insipid pallid glare of self-introspection.
Fundamental laws no longer exist beyond spectral grips.

Lowest frequencies of light no longer hiding from sight.
Deepest red floods implacably, mercilessly, seeping freely.

Whispers in the Wind
Jay Rose Ana

Further I fall, willingly, tetra-chromatically challenging.
Stripping me of materialistic things.

To the purest naked energy.
A single point.

Absence of colour.
Waves diffusing into infinite quiets of silent seas.

Tuning frequencies of the universe own heartbeat.
Quark to proton, to all that was.

To all that could be.
To face creation itself.

And demand.
No, beg.

An answer to a selfish question.

Why me?

Whispers in the Wind
Jay Rose Ana

Heavens Purse

When my time comes, and my atoms disperse.
And I do wend skyward to heavens purse.
Look to the clouds and beyond to starlight.
Wishing you well I shine in the night light.

Do not be dismayed that my time has come.
For I end my life as I had begun.
Happy and free and ultimately me.
At peace with myself as we all should be.

When my time comes, and my atoms disperse.
Hold out your hands as I gently traverse.
And guide me upwards to begin my flight.
I will ask the moon to shine bright tonight.

And know that I lived and loved in your light.
Happiness dwelt in your wonderful sight.
And life was all but a simple rehearse.
For the day we return to heavens purse.

Whispers in the Wind
Jay Rose Ana

Labyrinth

Life is a complex labyrinth.
Of twists and turns and dead ends.
New starts and unexpected consequences.
Illuminated through the hearts of friends.

Amidst twisting cryptic pathways.
Searching, we feel our way around.
Sometimes we stand ten-feet tall.
Sometimes we fall to muddy ground.

With hopes that one day, perhaps.
We may stumble upon the right paths.
Find, ourselves, waiting there.
Beside calm water, resting our wear and tear.

With humility, with compassion.
A bright smile, and welcoming arms.
For a life lived with hungry passion.
A loving heart and open palms.

Whispers in the Wind
Jay Rose Ana

Trust in your intuition, greet others
with charity. Share your path light,
and your journey will become the
destination, of you, as you take flight.

You are the light.
Be brave and live.
Your life your way.
Always shine bright.

And the labyrinth.
Will hold you.
No more.

Whispers in the Wind
Jay Rose Ana

Anonymity

As water is sure
   it is not ice nor steam,
whispers reflect
   a more judgemental scream.

Doubt is confused,
   minted spears, for words they mean,
used, and abused,
   like keeping front lawn grass green.

Weekends, we escape
   through silent meadows,
and wonder gleefully,
   at wild, verdant, beauty there.

Cut our own grass,
   back, into conformity,
Olive, viridescent,
   anonymity.

Whispers in the Wind
Jay Rose Ana

Turning Point

A signpost. A crossing.
A turning point in life.

Should she keep walking straight?
Maybe go left, or maybe turn right?

A sign, worn and tattered.
Sways gently in the wind.

But legs just keep on walking.
Penance, for a life sinned.

The path to the west.
Is falsely blessed.

The path to the east.
The sound of the beast.

The road behind.
Was long and hard.

Whispers in the Wind
Jay Rose Ana

Held uneven footing.
Potholes, every yard.

The road ahead.
Hidden in a haze.

But legs keep on walking.
Head, in a daze.

Let her rest a while.
At this intersection.

🍃

A pause, at best.
For life's deep reflection.

Whispers in the Wind
Jay Rose Ana

A Quiet Place

She wants to find a quiet place.
A place where each, and every, step.
Holds warmth of sand under foot.
A quiet place, full of friendly
smiles, acceptance, and holding hands.

She wants to find a quiet place.
To unwind and release a life.
Feeling she is not good enough.
Not meeting pointless criteria.
A life of conflict and strife.

She wants to find a quiet place.
It doesn't really matter where.
She need not even call it home.
Just a place where all life feels fair.

And you, are very welcome there.
In the quiet place.

Whispers in the Wind
Jay Rose Ana

Hell Be Warned

Millennia scorched; the planet did quake.

Melts earth, wind and fire amalgamate.

Spilling death with its smouldering wake.

Consuming all 'til no more to take.

Snow-capped prominent granite mountain.

Expunged, smelted to a molten lake.

Blistering forests; steaming fountain.

Feeds the beast, and even more to take.

The fiery truth, the cold-hearted lie.

White hot heartache; screams make mountains quake.

Whispers in the Wind
Jay Rose Ana

Burn love's hopeless feast in ashen sky.

Time and heat rage on and more to take.

Never quenched, blazing trail, all aflame.

Igniting passion with red-hot shame.

Charred remains from suffocated breath.

Incinerated through searing death.

Hell on earth, a passion and fury.

Nothing will restrain this scorned heart break.

So, lock hells strong gates and douse hells fires.

Hell hath been warned and make no mistake.

Never Fitting In

I tried fitting in

It never sat well with me

I listened to others

I never listened to me

Accepting myself for who I am now

I feel so much lighter

Accepting me feels like

Wanting so very much

To interact with the world

I tried

To go with the flow

It was hard to swim

Others swam with the stream

I swam against my dream

It always was so very hard

Shedding an old coat weighing me down

Learning to walk again, unable to talk

To pull myself together

And live again
For the first time

Whispers in the Wind
Jay Rose Ana

Live, Love

If today were that day.
The sunset of that final day.
In your last moments.
What might you regret?
That never quite got underway.
Or was put off to another day?

We do not know the
happenings of tomorrow.

Life is such a brief endeavour.
Racing towards the end of never.
Where our mist will hang.
For a little while.
But will disperse.
To heavens purse.

Do not wait until your final moment.
To tell someone you love them.
You still have a lifetime ahead.

Of every-days' to show them.

Whispers in the Wind
Jay Rose Ana

Sometimes

Sometimes it is us who are able to give others help and sometimes it is us who need the help of others

Giving help is often seen as strength yet needing help is often seen as weakness

Life is not so simply divided if we remember we are only human and ultimately exist for both

Book of Life

The book of life
rarely ends with
"They lived happily
ever after".

For that,
you will need
to have lived
the spaces

between the pages

Whispers in the Wind
Jay Rose Ana

Silent Voices

Why when it is quiet
Does quiet beget quieter?

And one by one
Silent voices hush

Until a collective sigh
Towards a distant sound

Instils the raucous rush

Whispers in the Wind
Jay Rose Ana

Your Vesuvius

The volcano erupted. It was abhorrent.

Destroying everything with its angry torrent.

Laying waste to all as far as eyes could see.

Thick with despair from highest sky to deepest sea.

The darkest April moon passed by the brightest Sun.

One by one stars blacked out as the eclipse begun.

Humans pointed skyward. Pluto covered its face.

Pluto cried in despair, shunned by the human race.

A spruce tree cracked, and fell, deep within the forest.

An abrupt end to a giving life so honest.

Whispers in the Wind
Jay Rose Ana

Scholars wonder still, did it even make a sound?

The simple truth. It will likely never be found.

History, as we know, revised and rewritten.

Truth of who did what forever remains hidden.

Whitewashed, scrubbed out, by the conquerors of lands.

Questionable deeds, washed away, by dirty hands.

Through tears of abuse, you built me your Vesuvius.

Your distant dwarf planet; your promises dubious.

Silently I despaired, I uprooted, I fell.

I am why you wash your hands; can you even tell?

Whispers
in the Wind

ACT THREE

interlude

Whispers in the Wind
Jay Rose Ana

Whispers in the Wind
Jay Rose Ana

Say No

I had to say no.
I am sorry but I did.
I like to say yes.
But need to put back the lid.

I had to say sorry.
I am busy today.
I am not able to help you.
In the usual way.

I had to say forgive me.
Please try again tomorrow.
I have tried my very best.
But my heart is filled with sorrow.

Whispers in the Wind
Jay Rose Ana

I had to stay silent.
Instead of sharing my strife.
For your sake not mine.
Mine is a tormented life.

🍃

I wanted to speak up.
I needed to share my pain.
But I am not that person today.
I did it once, but never again.

🍃

So, I am sorry but no.
It breaks my heart to say.
As much as I would like to help.
It is me that needs help today.

Whispers in the Wind
Jay Rose Ana

Memories

Memories make us who we are today.
Experience shapes us and never goes away.
For many years I kept them at bay.
Never being open, how I feel each day.

For a while there, it was touch and go.
I really could not decide.
If I had the strength to face my past.
Or keep the bottle top locked inside.

Seconds tick by, then hours, then days.
My love is long gone, took the easy way.
Over time, like oil, I spilled self-worth.
Wasted seconds, a wasted birth.

As the march of time went happily by.
All I could do was hide and cry.
Hating myself for all I had become.
Hoping for a sign from anyone.

Whispers in the Wind
Jay Rose Ana

It will be okay; it may take some time.
Your wounds will heal, you will be fine.
But standing on the motorway.
I was ready, to go, the other way.

A quick blast of a horn.
A screech or two of brakes.
In an instant I would be gone.
Who would miss me, for God sakes?

And then, one night, just driving home.
The penny dropped like a lucky stone.
All at once my demons rose.
And I felt much lighter in my toes.

Now, I am me, and time has shown.
With hope, and love, I was never alone.
For they stood with me along the way.
And gave me strength in becoming Jay.

Whispers in the Wind
Jay Rose Ana

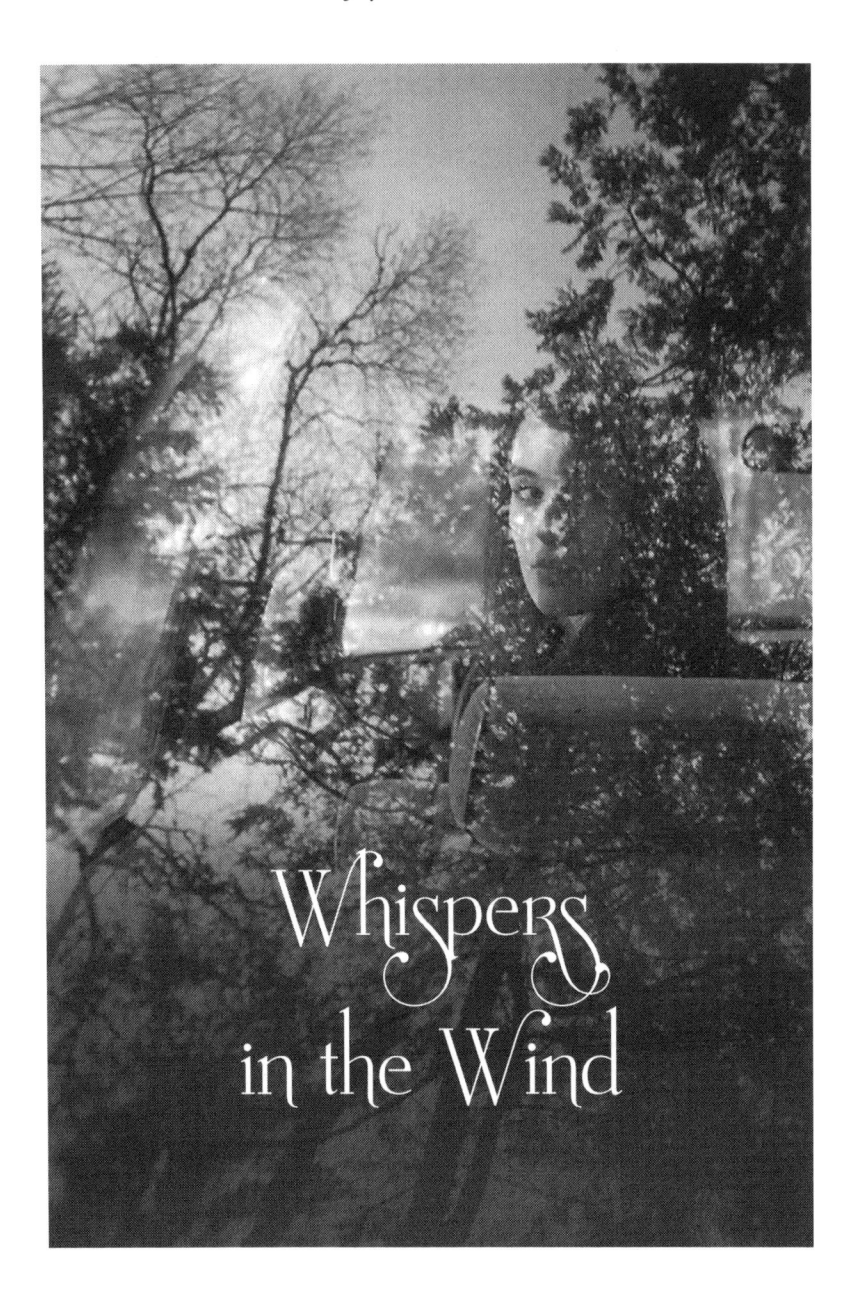

Whispers in the Wind
Jay Rose Ana

Whispers in the Wind

ACT FOUR

"yellow sapphires of hope"

Whispers in the Wind
Jay Rose Ana

I am seeking change.
Dear history, I free you.
I see tomorrow.

Whispers in the Wind
Jay Rose Ana

ACT FOUR

SUMMER SKIES	127
BRAND NEW DAY	128
YOU MATTER	131
BE KIND	135
NOT INVINCIBLE	136
HUMAN NATURE	138
PAIN	140
DESIDERATUM	141
BELIEVE	142
WHAT IF?	144
ONCE	145
SHADOW LIGHT	146
DOOR OF GOODBYE	147
TREES CRY	148
MOUNTAIN	151
WINDS OF CHANGE	152

Whispers in the Wind
Jay Rose Ana

Whispers in the Wind
Jay Rose Ana

she faced the challenge
like learning to walk again
unable to talk
yet wanting so very much
to interact with the world

Whispers in the Wind
Jay Rose Ana

Whispers in the Wind
Jay Rose Ana

Summer Skies

Fluffy sky hung out like washing on a line.
Clouds drip dry, as birds resign.
The distant rumble of a passenger jet.
Fuelled by hopes of a better yet.

The falling leaf, the seasons end.
Releasing the branch, starts to descend.
Life asunder, a crack of thunder!
A lightning bolt gives thoughts a jolt.

Blossom rests, love left behind.
Nowhere to turn, no one to find.
Cold, damp grass captures her fall.
The endless sky, an impenetrable wall.

Love is lost, above dreamy clouds up there.
New life marked by the sunshine's glare.
And even rainbows, looks down upon,
Its frowning sign, it is time to move on.

Whispers in the Wind
Jay Rose Ana

Brand New Day

Today is a brand-new day!
And to be honest,
I did not think I would see the dawn.

Engulfed in my own darkness,
I lay in the dirt, my life withdrawn.

Not even the light of the twinkling moon.
As I lay surrendered, life immune.

Despondent, and hollow,
one by one, between finger and thumb,
lay each bitter pill to swallow.

I had no more tears left to fall,
And I had no more friends to call.

Life's blackest night turned shallow grey,
hours of confusion, a surge of blue, then came day.

And in a briefest pause, between the two, I saw it all!

Whispers in the Wind
Jay Rose Ana

I saw the beauty of life itself,
through the grace of a shooting star!
So beautifully assured,
painting the sky,
with its magnificent trail so, so far!

I felt its connection as it passed me by,
and in that moment, I found the strength,
to give my own life, one more try.

With that spark, Earth held me close.
Winds blew away, my gathered dust, my lonely ghost.

Morning dew refreshed my repose.
And sunlight, that bright morning sun,
it warmed my soul.

I felt a jolt of life,
from my head to my toe.

And for the first time,
in a very long while,
I felt whole.

I heard a faraway voice,
from deep inside my mind.

Whispers in the Wind
Jay Rose Ana

Sit up, stand up, take a breath, be kind.
Accept what is done, pick yourself up,
get up on your feet, you are not giving up!

I push my hands deep into earth,
My fingers clasp dirt as I feel rebirth.
I have been as far as anyone can go.

Beyond the edge to the point below.
And just before those final feet,
I found the strength,
To take one step forward, and repeat.

I now understand,
the difference one small step can make.
A friendly hand outreached, an apology for a mistake.
I cannot change the whole wide world,
But I can live my life as me.

For, I am the change I seek,
and the world,
well, for today at least,
I am set free.

Whispers in the Wind
Jay Rose Ana

You Matter

You matter.
Right here.
Right now.
We have one life.
Most likely.
So, this is it.
This is the moment.

What are we doing?
What am I doing?
Right now.
To let you know you matter.

Are we doing?
Something?
Anything?
Useful?
Helpful?

Whispers in the Wind
Jay Rose Ana

Bringing Joy.
Or easing pain?
For someone else?

🍂

Are we standing tall right now?
Or are we falling again?
Or are we enjoying.
The temporary serenity.
Of nothing at all.

🍃 Bliss. 🍃

Embracing the moment.
Of silence.
To take in it all.
Then, do we try?

Something.
Hopefully.
Wilfully.
Purposefully.

🍃

After this pause.
Between moments.

Whispers in the Wind
Jay Rose Ana

To show someone.
They matter.
If for no reason, then…
when tomorrow comes.
They will look back.
And think.

I remember that moment.
I must mark that moment.
And show someone else they matter.

That is…
If there will…
Even be that…
Next moment.

Because there will come a time.
And most likely.
When we do not realise.
That we are in our final moment.
That is inevitable.

And so, this wonderful opportunity of life…

We have is finite.

Whispers in the Wind
Jay Rose Ana

Whatever we choose.
Whatever I choose.
Whatever you choose.
To do right now.
Matters.

Remember.
What we choose to do.
Right now. Matters.
Moment's matter.
Because people matter.
We all matter.

And the thing that matters most of all.
Are individuals.
Individuals matter.

They matter.
We matter.
You matter.

You are made
from beautiful matter.

You are beautiful.
And you matter.

… Whispers in the Wind
Jay Rose Ana

Be Kind

Be kind to yourself.
Be kind to others.
Be kind to creatures.
Be kind to our earth.

Be kind to the moon and to the planets.
Be kind when we set foot on Mars.
Be kind to things we have yet to understand.
Be kind to the Sun and the stars.

Be kind when life makes you angry.
Be kind when life feels unfair.
Be kind when you are lonely.
Be kind when dreams are up in the air.

Be kind when you feel sadness.
Be kind when you are able to share.
Be kind and set the example.
Be kind, be the one who is there.

Be kind.
Be the best kind.

Whispers in the Wind
Jay Rose Ana

Not Invincible

I am not invincible.

Because.

I hold onto hope.
Hope for better days.
That may never come.

I have love.
And offer it with compassion.
Wholly, without ration.

And I have heart.
A heart that can be broken.
By little words left unspoken.

I am not invincible.

Because of those things.

Whispers in the Wind
Jay Rose Ana

I am invincible.

Because.

No one.
Can tear.
Those three things apart.

I know.
Because.
They tried.

I thought.
A while.
I died.

But I, in fact.
Survived.
And you will too.

Hold onto hope.
Take heart.
And know you are loved.

And you will be.

Invincible.

Whispers in the Wind
Jay Rose Ana

Human Nature

I think it may be human nature.

When anxiety and fear are strong.

To start to question every little thing.

And fixate upon right and wrong.

Sometimes, I think, it takes a jolt.

A sign, perhaps, from far above.

That it may be sooner than we think.

To embrace those that we love.

And to not hold on to held regret.

And to give release to long held fret.

Whispers in the Wind
Jay Rose Ana

Because, I think, for all, our course is set.

Our legacy, a life of joy and not upset.

So, I think it may be human nature.

To share, to laugh and to love.

And to smile when we see a rainbow.

Amidst the hazy clouds above.

And to discover, what it means to be.

To sing, and dance, and wander free.

Then rest a while beneath the weary tree.

And close our eyes to finally see.

The beautiful potential of human nature.

Whispers in the Wind
Jay Rose Ana

Pain

I realise no matter
how much pain the
hurt feels nor how
far I
feel I
have fallen
that I
am in fact
feeling
something
once again

My heart still hurts
but I know that
my heart is
beating still
for the
first time
I feel
perhaps
I am
becoming
alive again

I made it through
you will too

Whispers in the Wind
Jay Rose Ana

Desideratum

We schedule alacrity by calendar.
Entertaining a notion for a day.
Tomorrow is somebody else's problem.
Yesterday's ad-interim is pushed away.

We have days for this and days for that.
Mired, pro-tem, in quotidian respect.
But this is a circadian rhythm.
That always happens to transect.

We wear, with zeal, bright buttons.
Ardently wave dusty flags from afar.
Maybe raise an impassioned eyebrow.
Whilst others, in vain, bear the scar.

Whispers in the Wind
Jay Rose Ana

Believe

Everything seemed impossible once.
But, amongst the impossibility.
One person found courage.
To believe in themselves.
To take one more step.
To give one more try.

All others doubted and
opportunity passed them by.
You have already made possible.
What seemed once impossible.
You are nature's wonderful creation.
Born with willpower to rise to any situation

You are beautifully immeasurable.
Never doubt of what you might be capable.
You are the inspiration for generations to come.
Generations who will doubt themselves.

Whispers in the Wind
Jay Rose Ana

Who might think it cannot be done.
Who will look to you to see what is possible.

The universe made you.
You are phenomenal.
You manifested your own reality.
From the energy of the universe.
You did the hard bit so believe in you again.
You already achieved the impossible.
Before breakfast.

Whispers in the Wind
Jay Rose Ana

What If?

What if everyone blamed everything on you?
And you, instead of standing tall, blamed you too?
What if everyone doubted the things you do?
And you, not trusting yourself, doubted you too.

What if everyone questioned, each word you said.
And their questions outnumber those in your head?
What if everyone hated you being you?
And hate seeped enough for you to hate you too?

What then of your hopes and your dreams, what of them?
What then of your thoughts and wisdom, what of them?
What then of answers to the question of you?
What then, with the truth, held deep inside of you?

What if you stood, when you fell, then stood again?
What if you breathed deeply and then tried again?
What if you trust you instead of needing them?
Held tight your dreams, never resigned them again.

When your reckoning day comes and be sure it will.
When they look upon you, will you hold your will?
When the questioner stands firm, ahead of you.
Will you shine brightly releasing love from within you?

Whispers in the Wind
Jay Rose Ana

Once

I remember once when you were here.
Memories once I gripped so dear.
Innocent times we once shared.
Young love we once dared.
I never once thought.
We would be once.
Loved you once.
Died once.
Once.
Once loved.
Once, we loved.
Our moment once.
Captured essence once.
Homeless once, forgotten.
Bottles top runways were once.
Once, you held me back here on Earth.
Hours and minutes breathed forever, once.

Shadow Light

on those days
when all around you
are dark shadows

take comfort
in knowing there
is light close by

on those days
when you see someone
surrounded in darkness

give comfort
be the light
that shines

Whispers in the Wind
Jay Rose Ana

Door of Goodbye

Standing in life's corridor.

In death's empty void.

The space between.

A moment to pause.

To hold a breath.

Before exhaling.

Composing.

And stepping.

Knowingly through.

The door of goodbye.

Whispers in the Wind
Jay Rose Ana

Trees Cry

Did you know trees cry?
Trees cry when stressed
And do we wonder why?

They scream when cut
But we don't hear it
Maybe we don't listen enough

Don't wait until
someone you know
is cut down

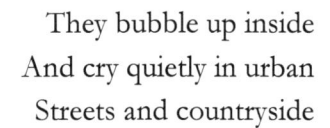

They bubble up inside
And cry quietly in urban
Streets and countryside

She wishes she listened
people are not so
different from trees

Let them know
It is okay to cry
on the outside too

Whispers in the Wind

ACT FOUR

interlude

Whispers in the Wind
Jay Rose Ana

Whispers in the Wind
Jay Rose Ana

Mountain

She toiled and climbed
the mountain
but never found
you there

She called and listened
for echoes,
searched for you
everywhere

The journey was
long and fraught
and took its toll
She has the wear and tear

And yet, she found herself
up there and breathed
for the first time
clean fresh air

Whispers in the Wind
Jay Rose Ana

Winds of Change

Punctual, at the river. Words fail, she feels a shiver.
Pausing to check for cover. Could this be a new lover?

A comma, on her page? Is she ready to engage?
Over the bridge she sees. A question mark over destiny.

She catches their eye. An emotional sentence.
Her heart beats twice. As they make their entrance.

Is this a promising new paragraph?
As they tread cautiously down the grassy path?

To the point of no return. Waiting for the page to turn.
There is nowhere left to run. Has this new story already begun?

Whispers in the Wind
Jay Rose Ana

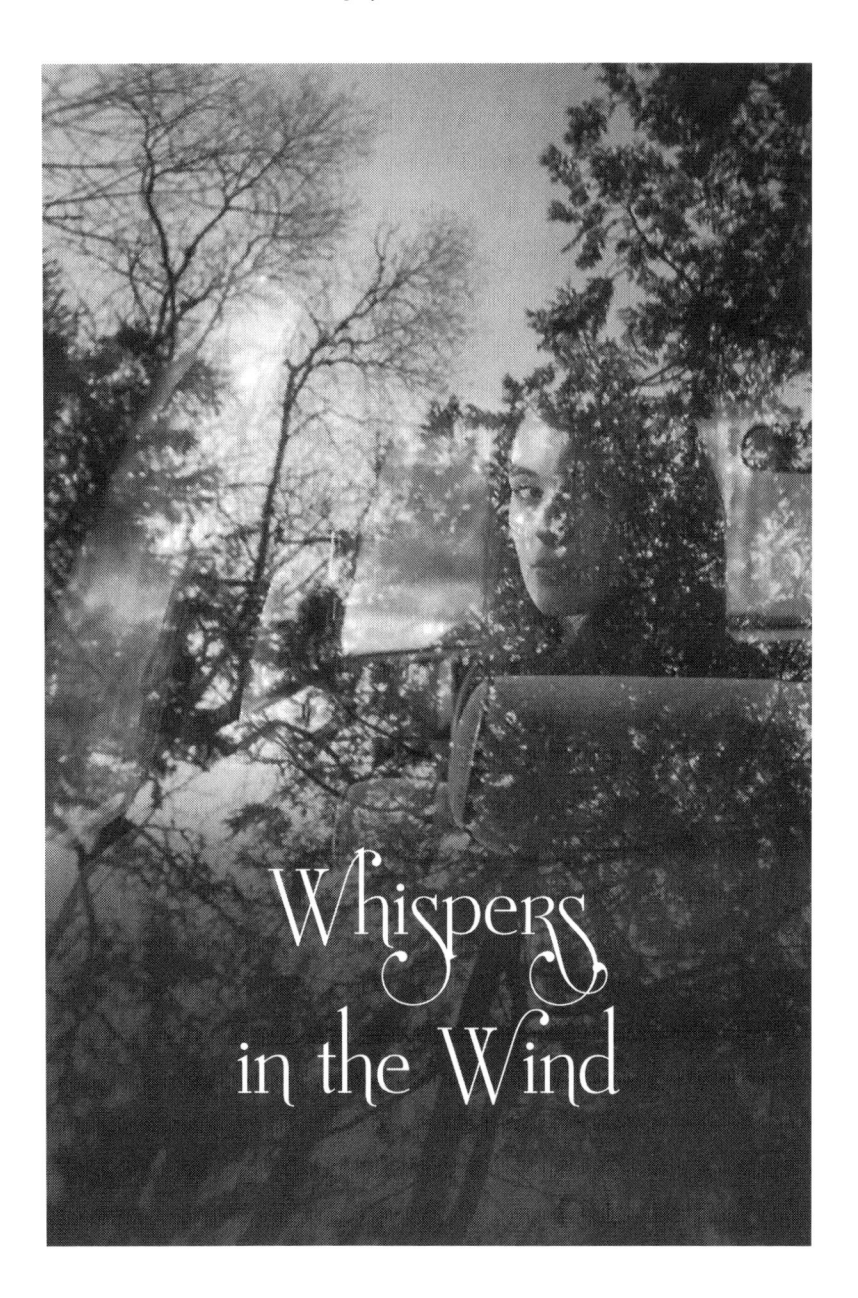

Whispers in the Wind
Jay Rose Ana

Whispers in the Wind

―――※―――

ACT FIVE

"green lights the way forward"

Whispers in the Wind
Jay Rose Ana

Breathing once again.
In the company of friends.
Finding new balance.

ACT FIVE

IMPOSSIBLE STORY	161
SO VERY FAR AWAY	167
THE SKY NEEDS TO CRY	169
WHISPER	171
SETTING SUN	172
YOU ARE GOING TO BE OKAY	174
WITNESS	176
ONCE MORE	178
SKULK BACK HISTORY	180
KNOW THYSELF	182
HELLO, I ACKNOWLEDGE YOU EXIST	187
THINKING NEGATIVE THOUGHTS	188
WALTZING IN THE GHOSTLIGHT	198
THE PENDULUM SWINGS	200
WHY ME?	203
ANXIOUS IN A SEMI-CIRCLE	204

Whispers in the Wind
Jay Rose Ana

Whispers in the Wind
Jay Rose Ana

she doesn't just survive
she is determined to thrive
she has seen it all
some days present a challenge
but she doesn't fall, she stands tall

Whispers in the Wind
Jay Rose Ana

Whispers in the Wind
Jay Rose Ana

Impossible Story

The story I am going to tell you.
Will sound impossible.
But I assure you, it is true.

I know, I was there.
In cold light of day.
I would be as sceptical as you.

This story has been sitting here waiting to be told.
But I always held off for fears of it growing old.
But I think now is the time for this story to be told.

Throughout my life odd things have happened.
Things that used to haunt and frighten me.
Things I could not explain nor could imagine.
Things I could not dismiss as phantasm nor fantasy.

But now I am older, maybe wiser, debatable.
And these same things give me strength.
Strength in getting through each day.
Each day of my life and they help in finding me.

Whispers in the Wind
Jay Rose Ana

But, please, bear with me, as this part of the story.
Does not yet sit well with me.
It is one of the hardest things to share.
I think, is one of those inestimable memories.

I had a friend.
When I was a teen.
Whom I loved dearly.
And I think, felt the same about me.

I was different then, shy, quiet, reluctant.
I lived my life introvertedly.
Unable to express what was on my mind.
Or anything really.

Growing-up, confidence was harshly stripped away.
Childhood took its toll and had not been very easy.

This person was like me, yet different.
Both, at the same time.
We made a connection, quite early.

We shared experiences.
And the rest…
For a while, we were writing a new history.

Whispers in the Wind
Jay Rose Ana

You see, they helped me.
When I was standing on the ledge.
Listened, and talked me away from the edge.

And they inspired me.
And I became we.

Not long after…
They died.

For much the same reasons, as they found me.
I survived, becoming their legacy.

Alone, I forced me to pick myself up.
Pushed my hurt deep down inside.
Locked away in the crypt of dust-settled memory.

It was the only way I could look at me.
Or bear my own company.
Or not cry when someone looked at me.
Reaching out for a hand no longer near me.

I existed.
Time passed.
I treated many an evening.

Whispers in the Wind
Jay Rose Ana

As if it was my last.

Many years later…

I was going through a hard time.
I couldn't sleep.
I couldn't stay awake.

I was walking a fine line.
I was drinking a lot of wine.

And then, one night, or early morning.
Whichever way you look at it.
Something extraordinary.
Impossible really.

They visited me.
I felt safe, right away.
Serene in fact.

Unafraid, why, I really can't say
But I know I was prepared to stay.
And before you ask.
Yes, my mind was intact.

I was never going to flee.
For the second time in my life.

Whispers in the Wind
Jay Rose Ana

Someone, could actually, see me.
Not just labels, virtue signalling, ideally.

Please remember.
I said, at the outset,
You would not believe me.

It's okay.
I know how it sounds.
We talked for hours.
They hadn't changed at all.

And yet, they saw me for
who and how I am today.
They didn't question it at all.

And once again I started to feel tall.

As the morning sun came up.
I briefly looked out through the curtain.
And as I looked back.
They smiled and faded.

A goodbye, I was certain.

They lifted me.
As I was about to fall.

Whispers in the Wind
Jay Rose Ana

And then…
I literally freaked out.
Struggling for breath.
I couldn't keep my emotions at bay.
The truth be told, I wanted them to stay.

And in that moment, I was ready to go.
"I want to come with you", I cried.
And I heard a whisper, "You have to stay, it's not your time".

And that was that.

It took a few days to carry on.
And to reflect that they had gone.
But surprisingly, I slept calm and well.

You see, I think they came to save me.
And to remind me, not to dwell.

I have not seen them since.
I am left with this unusual allegory.
And you may not be convinced.

But that's okay.
As this is my impossible story.

Whispers in the Wind
Jay Rose Ana

So Very Far Away

I count every hour, every one.
Every day since you have been gone.
You feel so very far away.
I think to follow every day.

I can't sleep, you sleep for us both.
Us forever, that was our oath.
I see your smile, in everything.
When it's quiet, I hear you sing.

Every day, I promise to try.
But tears come so I hide and cry.
My heart hurts so much, it may stop.
If I could, I would like to swap.

Whispers in the Wind
Jay Rose Ana

I was told the pain would end.
But it does not, it just extends.
I try to look forward not back.
Every time, my thoughts turn black.

I try to breathe, but anxiety strikes.
Cuts me down like the bluntest knife.
My sadness is rain.
Each raindrop, my pain.

I am no longer truly whole.
I am no longer in control.
The question always on my mind.
Why was I the one left behind?

Whispers in the Wind
Jay Rose Ana

The Sky Needs to Cry

I went outside to cry.
Looked up hopefully
towards afternoon sky.

Can you sky? Answer why?

Nimbus clouds lazy by.
I see it is the lonely sky,
not I, who needs to cry.

I release my torment.
Rain was drops of water
floating in oceans blue.

It is okay to cry.

Dreaming up to kind Sun,
shining beautiful truth.

Whispers in the Wind
Jay Rose Ana

Grey clouds drift on by.
Silent raindrops fall.
Refreshing Earths rich soil.

Take a moment for you.

Clear haze for better days.
Caressed by cool winds blow.
Blue skies reflect hopeful rainbows.

As I look far up high,
to clear blue, whisper I.

*It is okay to cry
my friend, I see your eye.*

Say I, I am you, sky.
The sky says aye, say I.

Whispers in the Wind
Jay Rose Ana

Whisper

In a whisper of air.
I knew you were gone.
Still breathing.
No longer there.
Staring blankly through the windowpane.
Lost thoughts, though your spirit remained.
Tucked away inside.
Locked in yourself.
Alone in the dark.
Only walls to share.
And as the light dims.
As moonlight begins.
It is reflected there.
In your hazel hair.
In a snap.
Like that.
You slept.
And I just
sat there.
And wept.

Whispers in the Wind
Jay Rose Ana

Setting Sun

The blackness sets in, who opened the door?
She made it this far, but she dreams of much more.
What help does she need? What difference would it make?
When the only courage she has is staying awake.

Sleep has left for days, crept out late one night.
Did not return, something was not quite right.
She turns out her bed light, pulls over the covers.
Longing to dream of times belonging with others.

Three in the afternoon, still laid in bed.
Chained to yesterday, tomorrow to dread.
Her bright spark expired, laid to rest.
All that remains, upset and stress.

Whispers in the Wind
Jay Rose Ana

Spiralling down foreboding steps of despair,
Rolling dice, in darkness, down there.
Hope is her cure, but it feels like her end.
Everywhere she looks, another dead-end.

🍃

Each day that passes feels like a mountain to climb,
If she can muster strength or does she give up this time?
Struggling for breath, she gently weeps.
No energy left for secrets she keeps.

🍃

But in the final hour,
A new thought sets in.
A ray of hope,
Could a new dream begin?

🍃

Can she let in new sunlight?
Open her full heart,
Brave the world anew,
Take a step to a new start.

Whispers in the Wind
Jay Rose Ana

You Are Going to be Okay

You are going to be okay.
Focus on getting through today.
You have already come this far.
Take a moment, think who you are.

Reflect, what you have overcome.
Think of all the good you have done.
You are going to be okay.
Take a moment, you earned it today.

It may take but a little while.
Though most worries turn out alright.
And, of course, think ahead to times.
Where you will absolutely shine bright!

It may help to find those people.
With whom you may connect.
Build a new bubble around you.
Listen with your heart and respect.

Whispers in the Wind
Jay Rose Ana

Maybe, set yourself a small goal.
Or two, perhaps be more proactive?
Give your mind a kind distraction.
Something physically active?

You might learn a new skill indeed.
Or explore your inner deep self.
Just do not shy and hide away.
Pick yourself up off the shelf.

Grant yourself a sense of belief.
Look back upon your life with good humour in relief.
Positive feelings are their own sense of reward.
Giving to others is a direction you could head toward.

Say thank you for something someone has done.
Spend time with someone, do not hide, do not run.
You have got this, it may not feel that way today.
But take strength from this, you are doing great.

You are going to be okay.

Whispers in the Wind
Jay Rose Ana

Witness

I bear witness.
I bear witness to you.
To your beautiful truth.
To your hopes and dreams.
Of who you are.

The birth of a star.
The eclipse of a moon.
The rings of Saturn.
The marriage of June.

From Eulers Formula.
To the Symphony Orchestra.
I witnessed all of these things.
But nothing is more precious to me…

…than you.

I gazed upon the glowing waters of Thailand.
I drew back the moonbow of Zimbabwe.
Saw the majesty of the rainbow mountain of China.

Caressed the Light Pillars of Russia.
Descended the Crater of Fire of Turkmenistan.
And plunged headfirst into the Pink Lake of Hillier.

Whispers in the Wind
Jay Rose Ana

But I surge with emotion.
When I look upon you.

I give you an ocean of Grand Canyons.
Walk your footsteps along the Great Wall of China.
Scale the dizzy heights of Petra.
Carpet the world in Japanese Cherry Blossom.

Then, rub beaks with the Puffins of the Faroes.

I do all of this.
To prepare the world for you.

I hold back the volcano that destroyed Pompeii.
Unearth a millennia of buried Secrets of Giza.
Paint pastel red the town of Tomatino.

Brave the Devils Throat of Argentina.
Lead the charge of the Stampede of Calgary.
And marvel at the Sunrise of Tikal.

I bear witness to your beautiful face.
To your soul, to your heart, and to your mind.

And I want you to know, there is not one thing.
Across all time and space.
More precious to me than you.

I bear witness.
I bear witness to you.

Whispers in the Wind
Jay Rose Ana

Once More

Why must the universe go on, without you in it?

Let the Moon come to rest, let the Earth stop spinning.

Let Venus freefall and let Mars collapse.

Let the Sun shine its final light, surrender Mercury with a gasp.

Let the stars all go out in a beautiful pattern.

Let Jupiter weep as it crashes rings of Saturn.

Let Uranus contract until it fits on a pin.

Let Neptune disperse as its gravity gives in.

Let satellites break free and drift deep into space.

Carrying the memory of our love released from embrace.

Ignore all lonely cries from the vastness of space.

Make room for Pluto, we are sorry, lift your head from disgrace.

Whispers in the Wind
Jay Rose Ana

Let comets collide as their icy trail shatters.

Let blackholes implode spilling out all that matters.

Let the Milky Way fade as one-by-one Solar Systems fall.

Wherever there is light, make it dark, blacken it all.

Let the edge of the cosmos slow time until it stalls.

As our dreams and plans now collect where they fall.

I would tear apart this universe. I would cast aside it all.

To see your beautiful face, look back upon me, once more.

Whispers in the Wind
Jay Rose Ana

Skulk Back History

It has been a while since you called.
For a short time there, History,
you really couldn't get enough.
These days, you almost never call.

I see you dancing with others,
as you once Tango'd here with me.
Whirlwinds of loving attention,
whilst I surrendered helplessly.

I learned from you, History.
I learned to weather your storm.
To always carry umbrellas.
To be me, not follow a norm.

Whilst you so tenderly caressed,
biting, gnawing off, chunks of flesh.
From innocent necks presented,
Unarmed, you left them tormented.

I see through your shadowy veil,
into your deepest blackest night.
You need to survive, History,
you skulk and prey upon their fright.

But can you thrive? I look back now.
History, you are built on lies.

Whispers in the Wind
Jay Rose Ana

I awakened to your darkness
History, somehow, I survived.

I have a new friend with me, Now,
It doesn't judge, it doesn't hold a grudge.
Is not filth through which I lumber,
try to move me, I will not budge.

My friend is Now and never leaves me.
To you and false prophets you spew.
I reject you dear History.
You and I, from today, are through.

I applaud you History, still,
please step up, take your final bow,
Then, slink back to where you came from,
For this is my time, this is Now.

Whispers in the Wind
Jay Rose Ana

Know Thyself

Laying down to sleep.
At the end of the day.
In the night-time hours.
Thinking the thoughts of life.
To reflect, face, and conquer strife.

To be strong.
Accept when we are wrong.
And do the right thing.
Sometimes relapse.
And fall.
And think again.
Perhaps.

Aristotle said know thyself.

Through knowing ourself we become wiser about things we stand for. The inner things, the deeper things. The unspoken things that guide us. And the hopes and dreams that beguile us, and the fears and insecurities that hide us.

Taking time to know ourself helps give life purpose and meaning for the challenges that are far behind us, and for all those unknowns that lay yet ahead of us.

Thinking.
Laying in our bed.

Whispers in the Wind

Jay Rose Ana

And trying not to make assumptions, of things, and of people, and to inform our opinion before jumping in. Because we all have things going on, but we don't always reveal them to others. Perhaps, sometimes, not even to ourselves.

So, be patient with others.

And patient with ourselves. Take time to enjoy small moments, and big moments, when we can. The small moments are the ones we remember most. And drive us to persist, in this crazy, mixed-up world, in which we temporarily exist.

A smile not a fist.
A hug not a list.

The things we overcome outnumber the things left undone. It is better to think of something as begun, and to have achieved one small thing, rather than none.

And fun.
Make time for fun.

And luck may happen, may play a small part. But luck more usually happens from hard work, and timing, and skills that we learn, and so persist with learning. For we never know when the timing happens, the right time, the time we can breathe. When we might otherwise hold our breath. Or leave.

Take a brief reprieve. If you need.

And that moment we breathe brings a moment of clarity. Perhaps charity, and we know, of ourselves, and trust. Sometimes without

Whispers in the Wind
Jay Rose Ana

clarity, in our ability, and with just a small amount of luck, we overcome, and we prevail.

And sometimes the challenge may be too great, and we may fail. But we learn more about ourselves, and our skills increase, and we become more ready.

It's okay to be afraid. Afraid of falling. Afraid of failing and of being afraid of being afraid. Overcoming things that we might otherwise be afraid of are times we learn and grow most.

Times, when we grow most of all.

But remain humble, work hard in silence, and the things we achieve will make the loudest sound of all. And will help others if they fall.

And they too will stand tall.

Because.

Actions become waves. Waves of sounds. Sounds that echo, like ripples in water, and they travel, and our success travels along, on those ripples, and echoes, and our failings too. But we accept those, as part of us, and we know ourselves. Because we turned our dreams into ideas, and our ideas into action. Action in ourselves, and there is little more powerful in our temporary existence than turning dreams to action, and feeling the reaction, of a single sound echoing through all of eternity.

Fuelling dreams of others who are just starting to know themselves. Showing them that strength lays within them. As it did us, and in doing so, we continue to grow, and the universe continues to expand.

Whispers in the Wind
Jay Rose Ana

Forever, into infinity.

Because we believe. And through belief we never really leave. We live on in the hearts and minds of those who receive.

We learn, through overcoming challenges, that we are able. No matter our physical existence. We believe, and we become what we believe, and we create the universe around us, and we become the universe. The starlight. Forever expanding. Forever discovering. Forever learning. Forever creating new challenges to inspire and drive us.

And give us new hopes and new dreams, and new ideas, to turn to actions. And it all happened because of you. Because you knew yourself, and you were afraid. But you did not quit, and you created echoes that created new stars. Checkpoints lit by starlight throughout the universe. Forming constellations, to guide new travellers, through their infinite dreams of time and space.

And we feel it when we feel the warm sun upon our face. Watching over the human race. The creators of dreams. Manifesting the splendour of everything we can imagine and more.

Life isn't always fair, but life is good. A gift, a trust to be cherished. As we are entrusted with creating the positive energy of the universe and warming the faces of others.

Of all things, of all times, of all places.

Know thyself, and though shall know the universe, and the universe shall know though. And life will be good. And it all happened right here in the present moment. That is all we have. So don't dwell, but dream, and act in the here and now, and make your spectacular mark on the universe.

Whispers in the Wind
Jay Rose Ana

The universe of discovery.
And know thyself through the starlight of others.

Laying down to sleep.
At the end of the day.
Under the covers.
In the night-time hours.

Thinking the thoughts of life.
And a little more perhaps.
You will know thyself.
And thyself will know you.

And a single ember.
Will shine.
For all time.

And the embers of all times.
Will shine as starlight.
Through the infinite expanse of the universe.

Lighting the way.
As you drift away.

Peacefully.
Into the dreams.
Of tomorrow.

Whispers in the Wind
Jay Rose Ana

Hello, I Acknowledge You Exist

Hey, you, over there! That glance you just gave me.
Well, I spotted it, and you made me happy.
A micro-expression, I think they might call it.
Please know that I appreciated all of it.

Your brief second of heartfelt emotional leakage.
Received. Morse code, if only I could speak it.
A tip of your head, a blink of your eye.
A slight upturn, of your mouth, as you passed by.

A micro-hello, over, in just a flash.
But your briefest glance, much more than a dot and dash.
It said, "hello, I acknowledge you exist".
A moment of hope that should never desist.

So, thank you, it is so awfully hard, I know.
When I appear very different than you.
To simply look me, directly, in the eye.
But we both laugh, we both love, and we both cry.

We are not very different, you and I.
And truly, this is such a fabulous start.
This beautiful fleeting momentary exchange.
A reduction in our chasm apart.

And I hope we can do it again sometime.
Until then, thank you, from the heart, to yours, from mine.

Whispers in the Wind
Jay Rose Ana

Thinking Negative Thoughts

People have thoughts.
All kinds of thoughts.
Thoughts that are personal and individual.
All kinds of thoughts.

And sometimes,
we have negative thoughts.
Bad thoughts.
And sad thoughts.

And that is how we come to think of them.
And try and deal with them.
A duality of thought.

Positive thoughts, good thoughts.
And negative thoughts, bad thoughts.
Thoughts we would prefer.
And thoughts we would rather not have.

And we seek to find ways to remove them.
Those thoughts that we would rather not have.
And we address them by saying things to ourselves, like,
"I only want to have positive thoughts".

And we try and focus on positive thoughts.
And we try that, and it may work for a while.

Whispers in the Wind
Jay Rose Ana

But the negative thoughts come back.
And the more we try not to think negative thoughts.
It would seem, the more we have of them.

So, we realise we need a bit more help.
And we head off to bookshops to buy self-help books.
Or we order them online.
Or read them electronically.
Or search the internet.

And listen to podcasts about positivity and well-being.
Etcetera, etcetera, etcetera.

And we work to try and prevent or remove negative thoughts.
And only have positive thoughts.

You see.

And soon enough we find.
This won't work.
This doesn't work.
It can't work.

Our brain and mind are often described as one thing,
the terms are used interchangeably.
And they are both strange, funny, little things.
And sometimes we describe them like a big computer.

And computers can be told what to do.
Computers can be told, programmed, how to respond.
And how to behave.
They can be programmed to work in a particular way.
And they can develop bugs that need to be worked out.

Whispers in the Wind
Jay Rose Ana

But those bugs can be fixed.
Or probably, more likely, the computer can be rebooted.
Switched off and on again.

And we wrangle with the thing,
until the computer does what we want it to do.

And the people that design computers,
know pretty much exactly how they will work.
How they will respond, the ins and outs, so to speak.
The machinations, the mechanics.
We can be pretty clear about that.

And we think that our brain, in some ways, is like a machine.
Probably a more mechanical machine with a big handle,
A handle that you wind, more than a computer.
What it does exactly is still not entirely clear.

Is it a storage device for thoughts and memories?
Is it a tuning device into some greater consciousness,
like a radio, in that big conscious universe out there?
Or is it a filter of some kind?
Like our own little pier connecting us to the ocean.

Who knows.
Really.
It is a rabbit hole of something we may never know.

Much of the brain seems concerned,
with how the rest of our machine works.
Our body.
Our body machine.

Whispers in the Wind
Jay Rose Ana

And it manages things like how and when our heart pumps.
How blood circulates.
How we sense things, using responses like pain,
to say, "hey, stop doing that! I don't like that."

But often we keep doing it anyway,
because we don't really know how our machine works.

We never really read the manual.
Or the instructions.
And we don't have access to the experts that designed it.
We can't program it.
But we know that it can learn.

And we can't really switch it off and on again,
when it starts to misbehave.
But we can be pretty sure of it.
Even though we still know very little about it.

Because, as far as the brain goes, we can see it.
Maybe not touch it.
But it is a physical thing.
And we know that.

But our mind is different.
It is not physical exactly.
We really cannot touch it.
And we cannot really be sure exactly where it is.

Because it is not exactly a physical thing.
It is not like a brain, or a teacup, or a bucket.
And we do not have a good understanding

Whispers in the Wind
Jay Rose Ana

of its fundamental mechanism.
Because it is not a physical thing.
It is more of a process thing.

So, let's try an example.

Point somewhere at where your brain is in your body.
Have you got it?
That was probably easy and you may be saying,
"This person is nuts, we all know where our brain is".
And that's good.

Now, point at your mind.
And where did you point?
Did you point at your brain again?
Is your mind in your brain?
Is your mind a physical thing?

Our mind is not specifically a machine.
I mean it could be.
Or might be.
But it feels different to us.
More than the sum of its parts.
And we cannot even point at those parts.

But we know it does not respond,
to being told what to do.
It just is.
It doesn't do that input - process - output type thinking,
like a computer or a brain.

So, we cannot apply rules to it.
We cannot program it,

Whispers in the Wind
Jay Rose Ana

or tell it how to work or behave.
Try that. Try it now.

Tell your mind to do something different.
Not your body. Not your brain, just your mind.

Close your eyes and try and remove a thought.
So, have a thought, say think about a cat or a dog.
And then say to your mind,
"Okay, I have had that thought, about the cat or the dog,
now remove it, I don't want to think it anymore".
And it is still there.

So, now try to tell your mind to stop thinking,
to stop having thoughts completely.
Tell it to no think of something.

Tell it not to think of, say, bells ringing.
Don't think of bells.
No ringing.
No bells and no ringing.
Don't think of it.
Put those bells out of your mind, so to speak.

If it helps, close your eyes and don't think of bells.
Do that for a few seconds and what are you thinking about?

Are you thinking? What kind of bells?
What kind of ringing? How loud is it?
Can you visualise bells in your mind?
Can you hear the sound of bells in your mind?

It seems the more we try and not think of something,

Whispers in the Wind
Jay Rose Ana

the more we think of it.

Isn't that funny?

We know that from the old tale that says,
if you cannot remember something.
Try not thinking of it.
And it will come back to you.
We are told that when we are young.
Or when we cannot find our keys.
To the car or the front door.

And if we try not to think of bells ringing the number of bells increases until we can actualise the sound of bells clanking in our head. Ding-dong. And it would seem, we are still thinking about bells.

Because there is no manual.
To the mind.
There is no guide.
And we cannot access the designers.

There only is.
The present moment.
The brain and mind and body.
Giving life and consciousness.

And it is a fairly well accepted idea that the brain,
and body are temporary machines.
Temporary vessels.
You know, physical things.
Flesh and blood and bone.
And when we are done with them.
Well, we bury them or cremate them.

Whispers in the Wind
Jay Rose Ana

We discard them.

We consider ourselves lucky if we reach a ripe old age,
where our body starts to wear out.
Eventually, the function of our body machine will stop,
and we will have determined that the thing we call life ends.
It may. It may not.
We think it may.
No one has ever come back and explained it all.

But what happens to mind?
And what happens to consciousness?

The likelihood is that mind is a part of consciousness, and that
consciousness is connected to something greater.
Something that connects us all.
And that sounds and feels reassuring.

"Ah, but!", you may say.
I cannot see or hear your mind and you cannot see or hear mine.
Only some representation of it through things we say, or write, or
draw, whilst we have that thing of life. Whilst our body and brain
machines are functioning. And we turn to someone, and we say,
"What are you thinking?" and "What's on your mind?"

And we are told, aren't we, when we are young, and at school, and
from professional people that we must not have negative thoughts.
That negative thoughts are bad.

We are told to get rid of them.
Push them out.
Stay away from them.
And only have positive thought.

Whispers in the Wind

Jay Rose Ana

But we just showed we cannot control mind,
and we cannot control thought.
We cannot tell them what to do.
We cannot tell ourselves what to think.

We can choose to not to act on those thoughts,
and we can choose to let them pass through.

We may be able to fool ourselves into blocking them,
temporarily, but not really. Thoughts will always come, whether we
are aware of them, or not. Like dreams. We remember some dreams,
not others, but we all have them.

And it would seem the more we try not to think of something,
the more it grows in our mind. Until we become preoccupied,
by these funny little things called thoughts.

And so, accepting them early is surely the way to stop them growing.
And so, accepting negative thoughts.
Letting them in. Not pushing them away.
Acknowledging them.

But not holding onto them.
Letting them pass through.
And they release themselves.
Before they grow.

And that makes room in our mind for other thoughts.
Some still negative.
But some positive.

And the positive ones we can let grow.

Whispers in the Wind
Jay Rose Ana

And let them in.
And try not to think of them.
To let them grow. Let the positive thoughts grow.

And those are the sort of thoughts that make us smile.
And we can associate the positive aspects
of our body to positive thoughts.
Like the muscles in our face, for smiling.
And laughing. And our brain, for remembering.

And hearing the bells ringing. Ringing with joy.
And happiness. And laughter.

And before we know it.
Negative thoughts are gone.
Because we thought about them.
We gave ourself permission.
To let them in.
Into our mind.

And we trusted our mind.
And we let our mind do what the mind does.
Because it just is.

So, sit back and have thoughts.
And don't worry about what kind of thoughts.
Because the more we try not to think of a thought.
The more it grows.

Isn't it beautifully simple?
Isn't it amazing?
Now, isn't that a thought?

Whispers in the Wind
Jay Rose Ana

Waltzing in the Ghostlight

I feel your sorrow
and I heed your call

I am ready to catch you
If you should fall

I stand here beside you
in the ghost light

Holding tight your hand
beneath the moonlight

I embrace you gently
as you weep

Hold eternity
the promise we keep

I am here with you
you are not on your own

You do not have to walk
this path alone

You do not have to walk
this path at all

Whispers in the Wind
Jay Rose Ana

My love is beside you
no need to call

Take some time
think on until daylight

I am here with you
each and every night

Our shadows dance here
under the ghost light

Waltzing together
until the first light

Take heart, no need
for you to fear

For I remain always,
for you, right here

Do not release
too many tears for me

For my love goes on
and my soul is free

Perhaps give tomorrow
another chance

Eternity can wait
for our last dance

Whispers in the Wind
Jay Rose Ana

The Pendulum Swings

when life is down
we can only frown
the stars seem dim
and hope looks grim

when we have seen enough
of the peak and trough
of life's complex wave
twisting how we behave

when we don't feel missed
think of our lips being kissed
and the warmth it brings
and the pendulum swings

free of friction
gaining momentum
its trajectory set
brings equilibrium yet

a coin has two sides
mornings long for evening tides
hope and time heal many things
life goes on as the pendulum swings

Whispers in the Wind

ACT FIVE

interlude

Whispers in the Wind
Jay Rose Ana

Whispers in the Wind
Jay Rose Ana

Why Me?

Why me?
So, I can be.
Be me.
Be what I see.
Live my life, free.

The whole odyssey.
All that I can be.
Living simply, freely.
A little tragedy.
All truth, no fallacy.

Just me, just the me you see.
The best, truest, me.
The me the mirror sees.
Truth beyond vanity.
The heart of sanity.

That's me.
That's I.
That's why.

Whispers in the Wind
Jay Rose Ana

Anxious in a Semi-Circle

Anxious in a semi-circle.
Looming slow creeping death.
Dry throat, thoughts encircle.
What truth must she confess?

This is a safe space.
No one will judge her here.
Nowhere to hide her face.
Visions of jeer and sneer.

Right to left, three before her.
Glancing rapidly at exit signs.
At least two may follow.
If courage bails and she legs it.

Two now, her heart is racing.
Hand and leg muscles contracting.
Inside, her anxious head is pacing.
Look around, sullen faces reacting.

Does she speak her truth?
Or save it for another day?
Will they demand proof?
Do she face her fear or run away?

She doesn't run away anymore.

Whispers in the Wind

EPILOGUE

"you are enough"

Whispers in the Wind
Jay Rose Ana

Happy, more alive.
Spending time with well-worn friends.
With a hopeful smile.

Whispers in the Wind
Jay Rose Ana

You Are Enough

You need to know this
If someone
has made you feel
somehow less

Or life
has left you
searching for more

Or you
feel broken
by events beyond your influence

Take a breath
To realise
You are enough

You are not less nor broken
Nor what remains from words unspoken
You do not need more nor repair
Nor words offered as empty token

You are enough
Perfectly and eternally
Enough

Whispers in the Wind
Jay Rose Ana

You found strength to make it this far
You found courage to look within yourself
You have wisdom of a life of experience
To listen to yourself when you say

I am enough
I am beautiful enough
I am clever enough
I am strong enough
I am good enough

There are only two real things that matter
Finding reasons to be happy
Maintaining your own positive attitude

Do not apologise for being you
Do not dilute your view of you
Life will not break you
If you believe in you

Raise your head and stand tall
You are capable and you are enough
Release yourself from
the expectations of others

Believe in yourself
You are
Enough

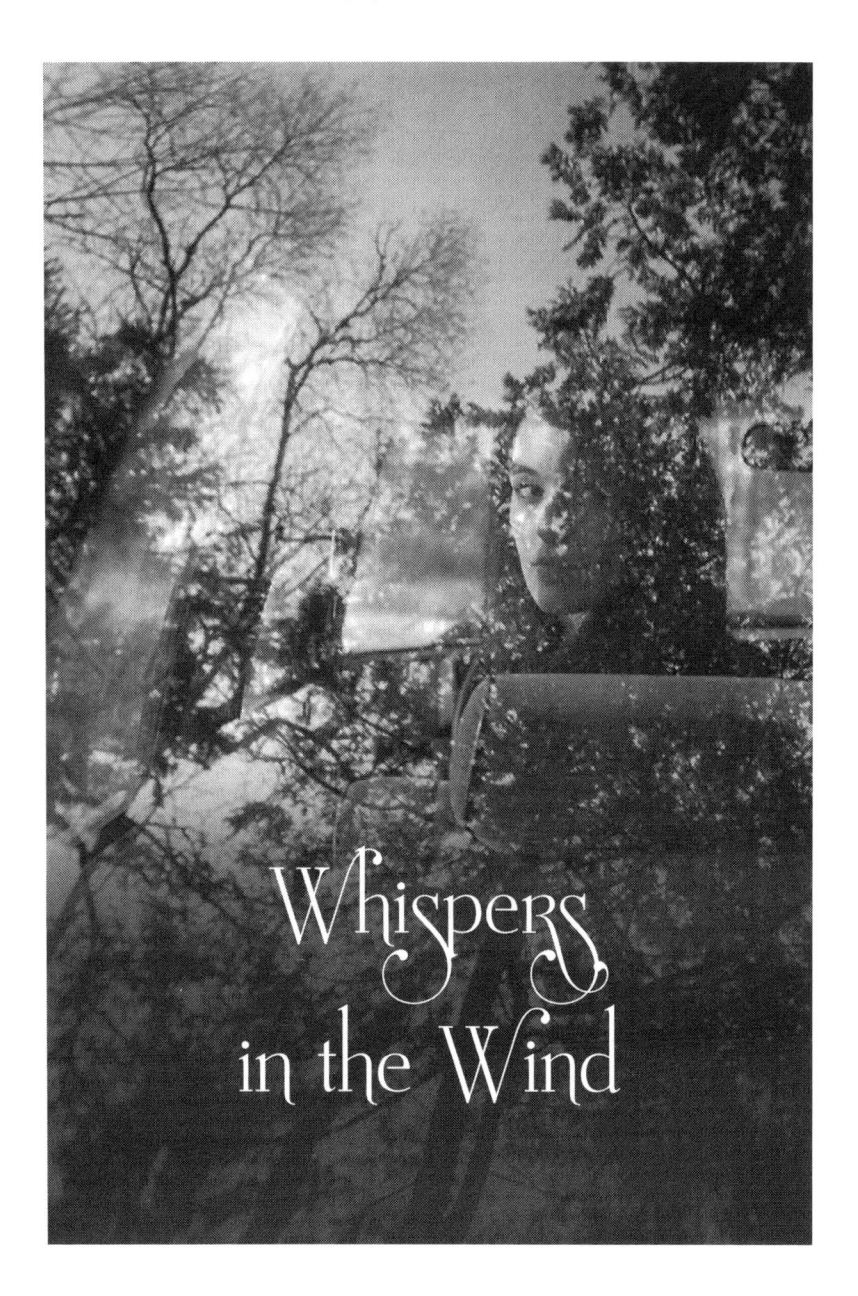

Whispers in the Wind
Jay Rose Ana

Whispers in the Wind
Jay Rose Ana

ABOUT THE AUTHOR

Jay Rose Ana is a transgender woman, mum, engineer, and poet from the West Midlands in the United Kingdom. Her poetry has been published in numerous anthologies, and one of her poems "My Journey" was played as part of the BBC Upload Festival 2021. Jay Rose Ana can often be seen performing poetry both in-person and online and she can be seen quite frequently in cafés and coffee shops where she combines her love of cake, coffee, and poetry. She can also be found on YouTube on her channel Jay Rose Ana's Thoughts.

Jay Rose Ana is the host of The Poetry Podcast and Words Collide Open-Mic which encourages first-time poets, and seasoned professionals, to come together in a safe space and share words in a supportive environment.

If you are interested in Jay Rose Ana's experiences of living her real life as a transgender woman, the good, the bad, and the downright unbelievable, seek out her podcast, "Becoming Jay", available wherever you get your podcasts.

Whispers in the Wind
Jay Rose Ana

A GIFT FOR YOU

If you would like to receive a free electronic book of specially selected poetry; together with an audiobook of Jay Rose Ana reading poetry, please send an email with the subject of:

WHISPERS IN THE WIND GIFT

To:
whisperingfree@minipoetrypress.com

We will also send you regular updates and bulletins to keep you up to date with Jay Rose Ana's new poetry, prose, videos and podcasts.

Whispers in the Wind
Jay Rose Ana

MORE POETRY

www.jayroseana.com

This poetry collection is also available in spoken word format, accompanied by music, see Jay Rose Ana's website for more:

POETRY AND PROSE
MOTIVATION AND INSPIRATION
MEDITATIVE STORIES
THE POETIC PODCAST
EVENTS including WORDS COLLIDE OPEN-MIC
BECOMING JAY PODCAST

Jay Rose Ana also has a page on Patreon with early access, additional poems, poetry, and inspirational messages specifically for patrons who support her poetry:

https://www.patreon.com/jayroseana

She can always use a coffee for inspiration:

https://ko-fi.com/jayroseana

Whispers in the Wind

Jay Rose Ana

FEEDBACK

Dear reader, I hope you enjoyed reading this book and I hope you found some of it relatable. In places it may feel a bit of a jumble and that's how it lived in my head. Whatever your thoughts I would love to hear from you. I would appreciate very much if you would consider leaving a short review either on social media, or an online book review site like Goodreads. A review doesn't have to be very long, but reviews are important in helping other people know about this book and let them know it is worth their time.

If you are on social media or want to leave a comment or shout-out it would be fabulous to hear from you, I can be found at @jayroseana and my pronouns are she and her.

Also, how many falling leaves did you find in this book?

Thank you and stay fabulous.

Jay Rose Ana

#stayfabulous
#whispersinthewind
#jayroseana

Whispers in the Wind

Jay Rose Ana

ACKNOWLEDGEMENTS

There are so many people I would like to thank. Firstly, you, dear fabulous reader, for picking up this book and reading on a little, thank you. I would also like to thank Out2Gether and the Standing Proud Writers Group, during lockdown 2020, for their support whilst this collection was being revealed week by week. The team at Worcestershire LitFest & Fringe for being such a warm and welcoming community to me. Holly Winter-Hughes for guiding my initial journey through her writing workshops. Martin Driscoll for being a fabulous advocate, designing the cover, and supporting this collection into print. Time To Change Worcestershire/Time To Change for supporting me and this book. Jemima Hughes, an outstanding and inspirational contemporary poet, who remains the only poet whose poetry can make me cry, together with Leena Batchelor and Rhianna Levi for being inspiring poets and kindly agreeing to read my collection prior to print.

My close friends who put up with me and keep me going through my diagnosis and episodes of Gender Dysphoria and Non-Epileptic Attack Disorder, I really couldn't do it without you.

The online open-mic poetry community for sharing their personal truths and inspiring me to share mine. Kate Justice and BBC Radio Hereford & Worcester for being supportive friends with me and giving my poems airtime. And for supporting me into BBC Upload Festival, which I consider a highlight of my poetic journey.

Whispers in the Wind
Jay Rose Ana

PODCAST

Love Poetry? Listen to The Poetic Podcast. Jay Rose Ana explores her love of poetry through coffee, cake, chat, and exploration of inspiring poets both historic and contemporary.

Available wherever you get your podcasts: The Poetic Podcast.

INDEX OF POEMS

A

A Dark Thought 32
A Good Place 51
A Guiding Hand 52
A Quiet Place................................... 103
All She Feels is Worry 75
Amber Fires of Heaven 93
Anonymity 100
Anxious in a Semi-Circle 204
Are You Okay?................................. 12

B

Be Kind 135
Being Different 83
Believe... 142
Book of Life...................................... 109
Bottletop Runway 21
Brand New Day 128

C

Chromatic Countenance 95
Cradle of Shame 29

D

Deluge... 62
Desideratum 141
Ditto.. 76
Do the Scars Show?......................... 38
Door of Goodbye 147

E

Everyone Dies Twice 43
Everything has its Place 40

H

Heavens Purse 97
Hell Be Warned 104
Hello, I Acknowledge You Exist. 187
Her Tortured Soul........................... 65
Hidden Treasure.............................. 33
Hopeless Hours................................ 23
Hot Air Balloon............................... 30
Human Nature................................. 138

I

Impasto... 63
Impossible Story.............................. 161
Instead, She Weeps 25
Invitation to Hope 71

K

Know Thyself 182

Whispers in the Wind
Jay Rose Ana

L

Labyrinth 98
Live, Love 107
Lonely Scream 61

M

Memories 117
Mountain 151

N

Nature's Kintsugi 78
Never Fitting In 106
Neverwhere 74
New Mornings Dawn 69
Not Invincible 136

O

Once 145
Once More 178

P

Pain 140
Pool of Tears 35
Portrait of a Best Friend 77

R

Relic 72

S

Say No 115
Setting Sun 172
Shadow Light 146
Silent Voices 110
Skulk Back History 180

Smiling Depression 22
So Very Far Away 167
Sometimes 108
Summer Skies 127

T

The Canvas Weeps 45
The Devil to Pay 66
The Pendulum Swings 200
The Sky Needs to Cry 169
Thinking Negative Thoughts 188
Time is a Healer 41
Trees Cry 148
Turning Point 101

W

Waltzing in the Ghostlight 198
What If? 144
What is Faith? 73
Whisper 171
Whispers in the Wind 11
Why Me? 203
Winds of Change 152
Witness 176
Words to Live By 84

Y

You Are Enough 207
You Are Going to be Okay 174
You Matter 131
Your Vesuvius 111

Whispers in the Wind

you do you love, stay fabulous

Whispers in the Wind
Jay Rose Ana

www.minipoetrypress.com

Mini Poetry Press